DENVER & BOULDER

# FISHING

CLOSE TO HOME

ISBN: 978-0-930657-51-2

Adler Publishing Company, Inc.
Phone: 800-660-5107
Fax: 303-688-4388

ADLERPUBLISHING.COM

# DENVER & BOULDER

# FISHING

## CLOSE TO HOME

# Table of Contents

The ponds, lakes and reservoirs in the Boulder/Denver Metropolitan Area offer surprisingly good fishing. These waters open up earlier in the spring than most other waters elsewhere in the state, so they offer especially good early spring fishing. Several lakes offer high quality fishing for quality sized trout and bass. Other lakes offer good potential for stocked trout, as well as the potential for trophy sized warm water species.

Fishing in and near the metropolitan area offers the novice angler a golden opportunity to learn more about the sport without having to devote an inordinate and sometimes prohibitive amount of time and money to the pursuit. Many of these waters are ideal for after-work, Saturday morning, Sunday afternoon, or even lunch-hour outings.

These metropolitan area waters also provide a perfect outdoor classroom for teaching youngsters how to fish. Many of the smaller lakes and ponds have good populations of bluegill and other panfish, as well as stocked trout that are not too hard to catch.

Outdoor Books & Maps, with the permission of the Colorado Division of Wildlife has expanded, updated and reformatted the original Colorado Division of Wildlife Fishing Close to Home publication. Fishing Close to Home is designed for use for the entire family and with the exception of certain dated information, the guide will be a useful reference to metro fishing for many years to come. A special thanks to the Colorado Division of Wildlife and all the city, county, and state agencies that contributed information included in this publication.

# Key to Symbols & Fee Information

## Key to Symbols

| | | | |
|---|---|---|---|
| Parking Area | Forest Service Facility | U.S. Highway | National Forest Area |
| Picnic Area | Fishing Area | State Highway | Water |
| Trailhead | RV Dump Station | County Highway | Trail |
| Downhill Ski Area | Restrooms | Trail Number | River or Stream |
| Boat Launch | Handicap Accessible | Forest Service Road | Primary Road - Paved |
| Bicycle Trail | Hunting | Mountain/Peak | Improved Road - Unpaved |
| 4WD Road | Campground | Colorado Trail | Unimproved Road - 4WD |
| Motorcycle Trail | Towns & Locales | Continental Divide Trail | Forest/Wilderness Boundary |

## Fee Information

There are no fees to fish most lakes and reservoirs in this section. Exceptions are: Colorado State Parks, Quincy and Aurora Reservoirs in Aurora, Union Reservoir near Longmont, Milavec Recreation Area near Fredrick, Boulder Reservoir and Arvada Reservoir. Fishing fees are sometimes waived for walk-in fishermen, this information is noted in the text. Local lakes and streams provide good training areas to teach youngsters to fish and sharpen your fishing skills. Both warmwater and coldwater fish are stocked during the summer months.

## Managing Agency Phone Numbers

Adams County Parks & Recreation ................(303) 637-8000
Agriculture Ditch and Reservoir Co ................(303) 987-2166
Arapaho/Roosevelt National Forest
  Boulder Ranger District ..............................(303) 541-2500
  Clear Creek Ranger District ........................(303) 567-3000
Arvada, City of ..............................................(303) 421-2550
Aurora Recreation Administration ..................(303) 739-6640
Barr Lake State Park........................................(303) 659-6005
Boulder County Open Space ............................(303) 441-3950
Boulder (City) Open Space ..............................(303) 441-3440
Broomfield Parks & Recreation ......................(303) 438-6360
Chatfield Reservoir State Park ........................(303) 791-7275
Cherry Creek Reservoir State Park ..................(303) 690-1166
Colorado State Parks ........................................(303) 866-3437
Colorado Division of Wildlife ..........................(303) 297-1192
Denver Parks & Recreation..............................(303) 964-2500
Denver Water Board .........................................(303) 628-6526
Foothills Metro Park & Recreation ..................(303) 987-3602
Fredrick, City....................................................(303) 833-2388
Englewood Parks & Recreation ......................(303) 762-2520
Evergreen Parks & Recreation ........................(303) 674-0532
Idaho Springs....................................................(303) 567-4421
Jeffco Open Space ............................................(303) 271-5925
Lafayette Parks & Recreation ..........................(303) 665-4206
Lakewood Dept. of Community Res.................(303) 987-7800
Littleton Parks & Recreation............................(303) 795-3700
Longmont Parks & Forestry ............................(303) 651-8446
Northglenn Parks ..............................................(303) 450-8720
North Jeffco Parks & Recreation......................(303) 424-2739
Pike National Forest
  South Platte Ranger District ........................(303) 275-5610
South Platte Park Ponds (Carson Nature Center)
..........................................................................(303) 730-1022
South Suburban Rec. District ..........................(303) 798-2493
Thornton Parks & Recreation ..........................(303) 255-7831
Westminster Parks & Rec ................................(303) 430-2400
Wheat Ridge Parks ..........................................(303) 422-2790

## General Information

General fishing license and fee information
..........................................................................(303) 291-7533
U.S. Geological Survey map sales. ..................(303) 202-4700
Fishing Report ..................................................(303) 291-7534

Campground reservation and addtional state, federal and city phone numbers on pages 10 & 11.

# Contact Information

NATIONAL FOREST SERVICE
www.fs.fed.us

APAPAHO/ROOSEVELT NATIONAL FOREST

| | |
|---|---|
| Boulder Ranger District | (303) 541-2500 |
| Canyon Lakes Ranger District | (970) 295-6600 |
| Clear Creek Ranger District | (303) 567-3000 |
| Pawnee Ranger District | (970) 346-5000 |
| Sulphur Ranger District | (970) 887-4100 |

GRAND MESA NATIONAL FOREST

| | |
|---|---|
| Collbran Ranger District | (970) 487-3534 |
| Grand Junction Ranger District. | (970) 242-8211 |

GUNNISON NATIONAL FOREST

| | |
|---|---|
| Cebolla Ranger District | (970) 641-0471 |
| Paonia Ranger District | (970) 527-4131 |
| Gunnison Ranger District | (970) 641-0471 |

PIKE NATIONAL FOREST

| | |
|---|---|
| Pikes Peak Ranger District | (719) 636-1602 |
| South Park Ranger District | (719) 836-2031 |
| South Platte Ranger District | (303) 275-5610 |

RIO GRANDE/SAN JUAN NATIONAL FOREST

| | |
|---|---|
| Conejos Peak Ranger District | (719) 274-8971 |
| Divide Ranger District (Creede) | (719) 658-2556 |
| Divide Ranger Distirct (Del Norte) | (719) 657-3321 |
| Sauguach Ranger District | (719) 655-2547 |

ROUTT NATIONAL FOREST

| | |
|---|---|
| Hahns Peak/Bears Ears Ranger District | (970) 879-1870 |
| The Parks Ranger District | (970) 723-8204 |
| Yampa Ranger District | (970) 638-4516 |

SAN ISABEL NATIONAL FOREST

| | |
|---|---|
| Leadville Ranger District | (719) 486-0749 |
| Salida Ranger District | (719) 539-3591 |
| San Carlos Ranger District | (719) 269-8500 |

SAN JUAN/RIO GRANDE NATIONAL FOREST

| | |
|---|---|
| Columbine East Ranger District | (970) 884-2512 |
| Columbine West Ranger District | (970) 884-2512 |
| Mancos/Dolores Ranger District. | (970) 882-7296 |
| Pagosa Ranger District | (970) 264-2268 |

UNCOMPAHGRE NATIONAL FOREST

| | |
|---|---|
| Grand Junction Ranger District | (970) 242-8211 |
| Norwood Ranger District | (970) 327-4261 |
| Ouray Ranger District | (970) 240-5300 |

WHITE RIVER NATIONAL FOREST

| | |
|---|---|
| Aspen Ranger District | (970) 925-3445 |
| Blanco Ranger District | (970) 878-4039 |
| Dillon Ranger District | (970) 468-5400 |
| Eagle Ranger District | (970) 328-6388 |
| Holy Cross Ranger District | (970) 827-5715 |
| Rifle Ranger District | (970) 625-2371 |
| Sopris Ranger District | (970) 963-2266 |

REGIONAL FOREST SERVICE OFFICE

Lakewood Colorado .................... (303) 275-5350

BUREAU OF LAND MANAGEMENT

www.blm.gov

Grand Junction Field Office ............... (970) 244-3000
Gunnison Field Office ................... (970) 641-0471
Glenwood Springs Field Office ........... (970) 947-2800
Little Snake Field Office ................ (970) 826-4441
San Juan Field Office .................... (970) 385-1207
San Luis Field Office .................... (719) 589-4975
Uncompahgre Basin Field Office. .......... (970) 240-5300

BOULDER MOUNTAIN PARKS .......... (303) 441-3408

CITY OF LAKEWOOD

Bear Creek Lake Park .................. (303) 697-6159

COLORADO DIVISION OF WILDLIFE

www.wildlife.state.co.us/swa/

DOW Headquarters, Denver ............. (303) 297-1192
Northeast Region, Denver ............... (970) 291-7227
Northwest Region, Grand Junction ......... (970) 255-6100
Southeast Region, Colorado Springs ....... (719) 227-5200
Southwest Region, Durango ............. (970) 247-0855

COLORADO STATE PARKS

www.parks.state.co.us/

Director's Office, Denver ................ (303) 866-3437
South Region, Colorado Springs .......... (719) 227-5250
West Region, Clifton .................... (970) 434-6862

U.S. FISH AND WILDLIFE SERVICE

Browns Park National Wildlife Refuge ..... (970) 365-3613

HINSDALE COUNTY

County Office, Lake City ................ (970) 944-2225

LARIMER COUNTY PARKS & OPEN LAND

Parks Office, Fort Collins ................ (970) 679-4570

LONGMONT CITY PARKS DEPARTMENT

Union Reservoir Park Office ............. (303) 772-1265

US Geological Survey Map Sales .......... (800) HELP MAP
............................ (303) 202-4657

CAMPING RESERVATIONS:

National Forest Service .................. (877) 444-6777

STATE PARKS

From outside Metro Denver Area .......... (800) 678-2267
From inside Metro Denver Area ........... (303) 470-1144
Note: Reservation period for State Parks, April through September.

# Fish You are Likely to Catch

## How To Catch Colorado Fish

*David Rye*

If you want to catch fish in Colorado, you must first become familiar with the various species the state has to offer. You should get to know nine cold water fish, most of which are trout, and six warm water fish.

Trout are more difficult to catch than many of their warm water cousins. Trout rely on sight to feed rather than smell techniques that are typical of many warm water fish such as catfish and panfish.

Trolling and casting are common methods to attract fish. Stream and river fishing involves the use of artificial flies and lures that can be carried by the current to fish in as natural a process as possible. Trolling is a common technique used on lakes.

Fish are one of the lowest forms of animal life. They have a relatively small brain for their body size. However, what they may be missing in intelligence, they more than make up for in keen eyesight.

Most fresh water fish feed at three basic times during the day. Morning feeding starts at sunrise and continues until 9 or 10 a.m. Feeding drops off until about noon when a short feeding frenzy will last until about 2 p.m. Late afternoons are the slowest time to fish. Feeding will start again around sunset and can continue into the late evening.

### Brown Trout

Brown trout were imported from Europe in 1883. They were planted in the streams and tributaries of the Colorado Rockies and have survived ever since.

They are one of the strongest survivors of the trout species. They can tolerate warm, muddy water that would kill most other trout. Browns prefer slow moving cold water that has lots of large deep holes. Brown trout feed mostly at night. They will feed early in the morning but will move to the deep water and pools at sunrise.

Most of their feeding is done on the bottom. Browns are aggressive trout and will eat just about any aquatic form of life, small swimming birds and mammals.

Spawning season for browns is in the fall. They will congregate in headwater streams. The females produce from 200 to 600 eggs in 10 to 30 feet of water.

### Rainbow Trout

The rainbow trout are one of the scrappiest fish in the trout family, and hence a favorite with fishermen. Rainbow trout were originally native to the West Coast. The rainbow was introduced into Colorado in the 1880s and has done extremely well ever since. In fact, about 75% of the trout caught in the state are rainbows.

Rainbows are notorious for being aggressive strikers. They are attracted to artificial flies and bright colored lures. They like lower, warmer waters. Rainbows spawn in the spring.

### Brook Trout

Many consider the brook trout to be the prettiest of all the trout. Their body is distinguished by sidemarkings: red and white spots on a dark green background.

### Mackinaw Lake Trout

The Mackinaw can be found in many of Colorado's deep, cold water lakes. It is by far the largest trout in Colorado's trout inventory. Angler's consistently catch Mackinaw in excess of 60 pounds.

Mackinaw are the most difficult trout to catch because they spend most of the year in deep water. When we say deep water, we are talking depths in excess of 60 feet. They move to the shallow water to feed in the early spring, right after "ice-off' and in the fall to spawn, which is the best time to catch these fish.

Most are caught on deep rigged trolling gear. They will also hit salmon eggs that are cast from shore or dropped from a boat. Winter ice fishermen attach sucker meat to Airplane jigs dropped to 60-plus feet to successfully catch Mackinaw.

Whole dead suckers also work just as well during the spring and summer. Weight the sucker to help get it down near the bottom where you want it.

The next step is to rig the sucker like an artificial plug. This is accomplished by attaching two No. 2 or 4 treble hooks to the front and posterior of the sucker. The hooks can be either tied onto the sucker or you can use a needle to thread the line through the sucker and attach the hooks to the end of the line.

### Kokanee Salmon

Kokanee are land locked pacific sockeye salmon. They were introduced into Colorado in the early fifties and inhabit many of the same lakes that are popular with trout fishermen. Kokanee will often be taken while fishing for trout. They will go after all of the popular trout lures and are equally fond of their own salmon eggs and other common trout baits.

These fish like to surface feed during the day. They will move down to deep water at night and move back up to the surface at sunrise. Most kokanee are taken when trolling. Spawning begins in October and runs through December. The fish school up in the tributaries that flow out of their home lakes. Colorado allows fishermen to snag kokanee with weighted treble hooks during the spawning run.

### Bluegill

Bluegills were introduced to Colorado in the early 1920's. They abound in many of the state's lower lakes and streams and are considered a primary food source for trout and bass. They offer fishermen fast paced fishing action and are excellent eating.

They are particularly active in the early morning hours and late evening. Favorite baits are worms and small dry flies. Bluegill like to feed in shallow water. However, as the water warms up in the later summer season, they will move down to deeper water.

Spawning season begins in the spring and continues until late August. Nests are built in colonies by the male of the species who also guards their spouse's nest.

### Walleye

Walleye are the largest member of the perch family and can be found in many of Colorado's larger reservoirs. A typical walleye will run anywhere from 2 to 10 pounds.

The name walleye was derived from the large bulging eyes that are a dominant characteristic of this fish. Their eyes are very sensitive to light. As a result, they will move down into deep water as soon as the morning sun hits the water surface.

Walleye feed at night. They will prowl the shoreline in

search of minnows, their favorite food. Casting in the dark with artificial or live minnows is the best way to catch these fish. Spawning begins in the early spring.

### Perch

Perch are relatively small fish that rarely exceed a pound. They are found in many of Colorado's warm water reservoirs and live in schools. They will spend most of the day in deep water. As evening approaches, they will move into shallow water to feed.

The best time to catch perch is from noon into the evening. For best results, fish a foot or two off the bottom with small flies, lures or natural baits. Perch spawn in the spring.

### Crappie

Crappies were introduced into Colorado waters in the 1880's and prefer the warmer reservoirs. They like to gather in schools around submerged brush and rock areas. During the summer months they will stay in about 8 to 15 feet of water.

Live minnows with a bobber are one of the most popular ways to fish for Crappie. Fishing for crappie requires sensitive tackle, to be successful. A small spin cast bubble can work better than a standard bobber. The line can be slipped through the center of the bubble, and you can add water to the inside of the bubble to improve casting distances. A light hitting crappie will be less likely to drop the bait if it doesn't feel the initial pull of the bubble.

### Catfish

Catfish are native to Colorado and inhabit many of the states warmer reservoirs and rivers. These fish like to feed at night. Natural baits such as night crawlers, crayfish, chicken livers or scented dough balls catch most catfish.

Catfish can grow in excess of 50 pounds. Most will average between 2 and 5 pounds. Catfish have a keen sense of smell which is the reason they will go after odorized bait.

Catfish move out of the reservoirs and into the spillway canals during Colorado's irrigation season, which starts in the late spring. They like the moving water and find plenty of feed in the run off.

Look for the deeper pools to fish. Cast minnows with enough weight to carry them to the bottom. If the cats are there, you'll hook-up within 15 minutes. If you get no immediate action, move on to the next pool.

### Bass

Bass are a member of the sunfish family and enjoy the reputation of being furious fighters when hooked. The two species of bass that are prevalent in Colorado are the large and small mouth bass. Largemouth were introduced into the state in the late 1800's. Smallmouth were introduced in the early 1950's.

Largemouth are larger than their smallmouth cousin. Adults will weigh up to 10 pounds or more. A typical smallmouth will average about 2 pounds.

Bass prefer shallow weed infested lakes. Bass action begins to heat up in late spring, just before the spawn. Bass become very aggressive and hungry during spawning. They can be found cruising the shoreline for food in the early morning and late evening hours. Casting and spin fishing are the best ways to catch a bass.

An important point to remember about bass is that they will adjust to the sun reflections on the water by changing their swim depth. The higher the sun's intensity, the deeper the depth that you will find bass.

Start shallow and work incrementally into deeper water. You are bound to find bass sooner or later. Once you get your first hit mark the depth that you were at. The rest of the bass will be at that same level.

### Northern Pike

Next to Minnesota, Colorado is one of the better pike fishing states in the nation. Pike were imported into the state in the mid 1950s to help control a rising sucker population in many lakes. Unfortunately, the pike developed an appetite for trout and left the suckers alone.

A mature pike will weigh anywhere from 3 to 15 pounds. They like shallow water with abundant vegetation. However, they will move into deeper water during extremely warm or cold weather.

The best time to catch a pike is in late spring, right after ice off. Most pike are caught casting big spoons and plugs into the shallow water near weed beds. Attach 6 to 8 inches of steel leader to 10 to 20 pound test line.

If possible, wade into the weeds and cast at different angles out into the open water. Retrieve the plug or spoon just over the top of the weeds. If you get a missed strike, stop reeling for a few seconds. Pike have a tendency to want to continue an attack a second time.

## Fly Fishing Basics

*David Rye*

Any fish, when hooked by a fly, will offer you some exciting action that can not be duplicated by any other type of fishing. A trout will rarely swallow an artificial fly as he does if caught with natural bait. They are typically hooked lightly through the lip by a relatively small hook. As a result, they must be carefully played until netted.

About 90% of a trout's diet consists of aquatic insects. That is why they are by far the most popular fish to go after with artificial flies. There are four categories of artificial flies. Each requires a different technique to effectively lure a trout onto your line.

### Dry Flies

The dry fly, as its name suggest, floats on the water. As a result, trout will rise to the surface to attack a dry fly. You literally have a split second of reaction time to set the hook. Dry flies are cast upstream and allowed to float in a natural pattern in and out of suggested trout holding spots. Getting the right cast into or near the right spot requires patience and plenty of practice.

### Wet Flies

Wet flies are fished just below the surface. These are fished downstream and slowly retrieved to simulate a swimming insect. There are 4 popular patterns to fish in Colorado. They are the Black Gnat, March Brown, Quill Gordon and Royal Coachman.

### Nymphs

Nymphs are fished on the bottom of the stream and in their artificial state, have been designed to simulate insect larvae.

The key to successful nymph fishing is to drift the bug along the bottom as though the current had turned up a rock and washed the nymph into the main stream. That is the action that trout are watching for.

The big difference in fishing with nymphs versus dry or wet flies is that you can't see your lure or the fish when a strike occurs. The only strike indication that you will get will be when your line suddenly stops drifting. At that instant, set the hook.

### Streamers

Streamers are designed to simulate wounded minnows and insects that may have fallen into the water by accident such as a grasshopper. Streamers are cast down stream or across the water. Retrieve the line in short jerky motion to imitate a wounded minnow or swimming surface bug.

### Tactics And Approach

The presentation of the fly is the most important skill that a fly fisherman can develop. You must learn how to show your artificial fly to a trout in such a manner that it appears real.

If the real flies are quietly floating on the surface, follow that pattern with a dry fly. If the organisms are darting around just below the surface, switch over to wet flys, nymphs or streamers.

Study the water carefully to determine the best approach to reach possible feeding fish. Feeding trout generally hold in one position and take insects that pass through their line of sight.

Casting up and across a stream is one popular approach to reach a trout's feeding lane. The cast is placed above and just to the side of where you believe the trout are feeding. This action avoids casting your line on top of feeding fish which would tend to startle them. The object is to allow the fly and leader only to float past the fish. This technique works best in evenly flowing water without strong currents to pull on the line.

Uneven currents pulling on fly line causes "drag" or movement of the fly across the stream. Drag is not desirable if the natural flies are landing quietly on the surface and your fly is skimming across the surface.

One way to avoid drag in strong currents is to cast your fly into the feeding lane. As soon as the fly settles on the surface, lift the tip of the rod. Allow extra line to slip through the guides to act as surplus line for the current to play with.

Fishermen that are unfamilar with the area they choose to fish should visit a local fly shop or sporting goods store. "Locals" are experts on seasonal hatchs and hot spot fishing areas. They can provide you with the flies, etc., needed to be successful.

---

## Taking Care of the Catch

*Nebraska Game & Fish*

Fresh fish is extremely perishable. Any fish left in the hot sun can spoil in less than an hour. Regardless of how you are going to prepare your fish, your fish needs taken care of from the minute you catch the fish until it reaches the cook. Consider catch and release if you are not prepared to care for the catch.

It is best if the fish is killed immediately, cleaned and placed on ice. If you can not clean the fish immediately keep it cool and clean it within a few hours. This will reduce the chance of spoilage in warm weather and improve the table quality of the catch.

**The following methods can be used to freeze the fish:**

• **Freezer wrapping:** Package meat sized packages. You can use heavy duty aluminum foil, plastic freezer proof wrap or plastic bags. It is important with any of these wrappings to remove all the air and seal tightly.

• **Glazing:** This is achieved by dipping frozen fish in ice water and letting it freeze between coating. Do this until you have a good coat of ice over the entire fish.

• **Block freezing:** Simply freeze the fish in a solid block of ice.

• **Label and date your packages:** Fish properly wrapped will keep for 3-6 months and retain its good flavor and quality. Thawing fish in the refrigerator, keeping it covered, is the best method for preparing the catch for the frying pan or broiler. However, fish also can be thawed with cold running water or using a microwave oven. Taking steps to protect your catch will reward you with a dinner well worth the time and effort.

## SPIN FISHING

David Rye

Spin fishing is the art of casting line a relatively significant distance to entice fish to hit a variety of food options including lures and natural baits. It has become one of the more popular ways to fish Colorado waters since spin casting does not require extensive training. You still need the skill of knowing where to fish, and what lure or bait to use.

A visit to the local tackle shop can circumvent this problem. Chances are, the local boys already know what the fish are hitting and will share this information with you.

### TROLLING

For boat owners, trolling is a great way to fish. There are four key elements that make up successful trolling; proper trolling speed, type of water fished, equipment used, and most important, the depth of water fished.

Fish are more comfortable and numerous at certain water temperatures. As the sun and weather conditions change during the course of the day, different species of fish will seek different water levels.

Measure the temperature of the water before you set your trolling depth. Change trolling depths on a regular basis until you hit on where the fish are. Some fishermen use fish finders to eliminate the guesswork of locating fish.

### LURES

In recent years lures and especially plugs that make noise have become increasingly popular. A number of the professional bass tournament fishermen use them with consistent success in attracting fish.

Propeller lures have been around for a long time. They are made up of a plug that has been equipped with a metal propeller mounted in the front or in the back. They are designed to make a splashing noise when retrieved.

Regardless of what you use, the idea is to make your lure imitate whatever it was designed to look like. If it is a bait fish, it should act like a wounded minnow. Artificial frogs and crayfish should act like those organisms.

The science of fishing with lures requires some experimentation. Some fish will respond to a slow, steady retrieve. At other times, they may respond to a fast, erratic retrieve. Vary your retrieve tactics until you hit on the right combination.

### PLUGS

Most plugs have been designed to simulate surface swimming organisms such as frogs, crayfish and even mice. If a plug doesn't attract any hits, you have two basic choices. Either change to another plug or change the action of your favorite lure. Adjusting the diving lip of the plug with pliers can vary plug action. Most plugs are manufactured to perform a deep dive or simulate a swimming organism.

If the lip is bent down slightly, you can control the depth of the dive. A diving plug can be changed to a surface splasher and popper by bending the lip at a 90-degree angle from the face of the plug. Don't be afraid to try different angles until you hit upon the right combination.

### JIGS

Jigs are designed to sink to the bottom when cast. The rod is jerked upward to pull the jig about a foot off bottom. The slack line is then taken in while the jig is allowed to return to the bottom. The process is repeated until you get a hit or run out of line. Variations in the retrieve such as quick and slow jerks and retrieves can all add up to getting strikes. The idea is to simulate a frantic bait fish.

Although most jigs do not look like bait fish, they have been used over the years to successfully bring in big fish. If you are fishing with a partner who is also using a jig, try casting both jigs in the same area. Fish tend to be attracted to schools of bait fish. In this case, two jigs retrieved together may entice the fish to move into what they think is a school.

Jigs are available in a wide range of weights, sizes and shapes. The head is typically made of lead with a hook that protrudes out and curves above the head. They can be purchased with and without any dressing on the hook. Undressed jigs can be baited with natural baits such as night crawlers, salmon eggs or of pork rinds. The dressed version comes in a variety of options. Most have feathers that extend out from the head and cover the hook.

Dressed jigs come in a variety of colors. The light colors such as white and yellow are used to simulate bait fish. The darker colors (reds and greens) can be used to help add contrast to the color of the bottom. If the bottom conditions are a light sandy color, a darker color may stand out better than a light color.

### PLASTIC WORMS

Many veteran fishermen consider the plastic worm the deadliest of all the artificial lures. They are particularly potent for taking bass. They come in a variety of colors, sizes and shapes. As shown in the illustration that follows, worm rigs can be as simple as a plastic worm draped over a hook or as elaborate as having spinners and feathers trailing the head.

Before you start fishing, get acquainted with the worm rig that you have selected. Cast it out into some shallow water where you can see your worm. Note that the weighted head will take it to the bottom leaving the lighter tail to float and wave naturally in the current.

As you begin a slow retrieve, the leaded head will stay on the bottom and kick up mud giving the appearance that the worm is grubbing or feeding. That is the proper action that you want to simulate.

Now for the cast. You may get a strike as soon as the worm hits the surface or before it reaches the bottom. Strikes in this stage are usually very hard and you should set the hook immediately.

The reverse is usually true when you're fishing along the bottom in the manner previously described. You must learn how to distinguish between a tap that is felt from dragging along the bottom and a legitimate strike.

If you are not sure, allow some line to come freely off your reel. If a fish has your worm in its mouth, the line will start to move away in the direction that the fish has elected to swim. When you feel some tension on the line set the hook.

# Reference Map

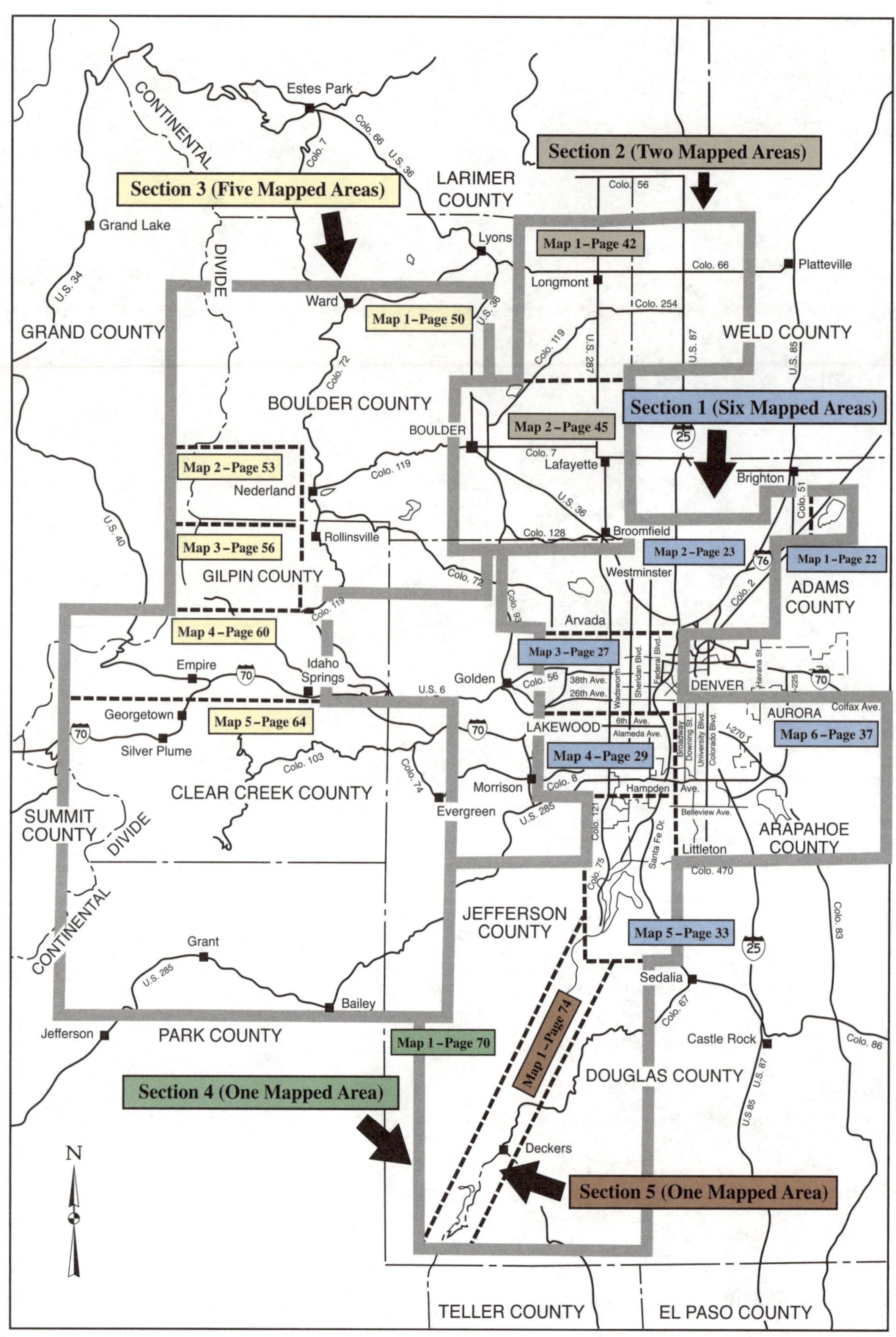

# List of Front Range Fishing Locations

## Section 1

# Metro Denver Area

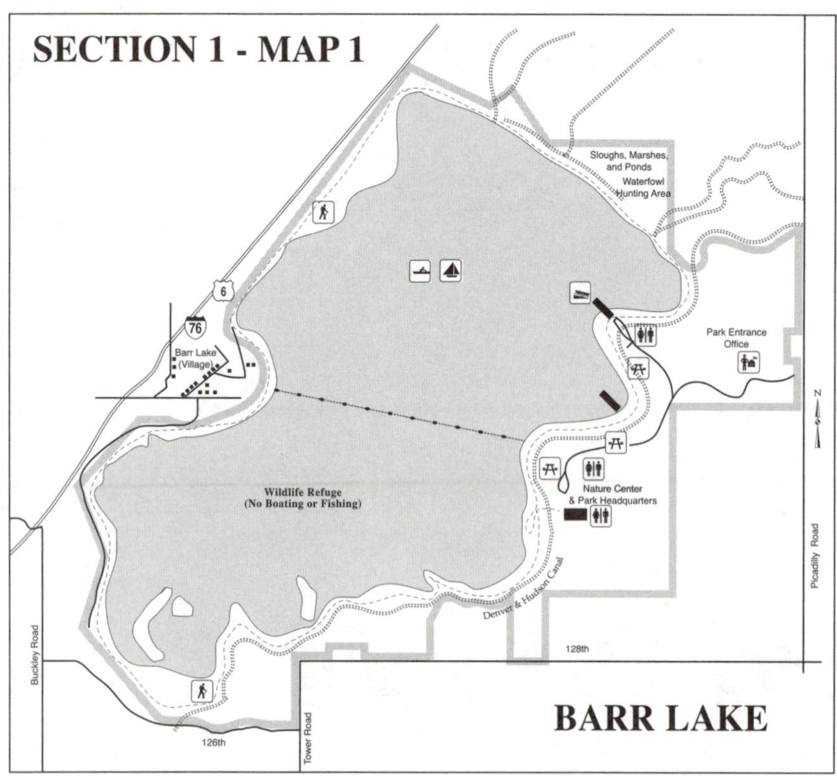


## 1 Barr Lake State Park

**Location:** North of 128th Ave. between Interstate 76 and Picadilly Road. Northeast of Denver off I-76. East on Bromley Lane to Picadilly Road, then south on Picadilly to park entrance. Parking areas are on the east side of lake.
**Size:** 1,900 acres; 42 feet maximum depth.
**Fish:** Carp, channel catfish, crappie, largemouth bass, smallmouth bass, rainbow trout (catchable-sized stocked) sucker, yellow perch, wiper and tiger muskie.
**Agency:** Colorado State Parks.
**Comments:** Open 5 a.m. to 10 p.m. Motor boats 10 HP or less. No boating in the wildlife refuge. Fee area with free walk-in access. Premier carp and channel catfish fishery. Extreme water level fluctuation. No fishing from dam. May close due to capacity. Boat ramp on east side by parking area. Nature center & trails.
Eagle and wildlife viewing area.

Horseback riding on Barr Lake

One of many picnic areas at Barr Lake State Park

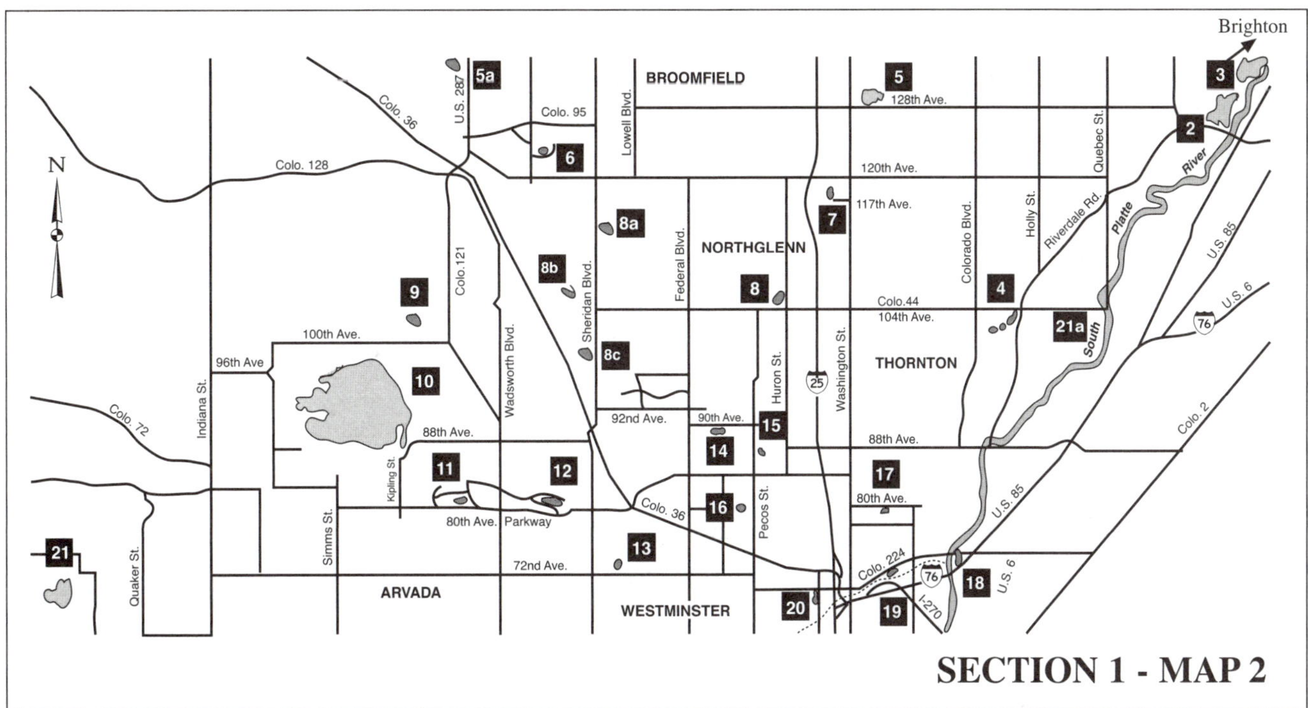


## 2 Adams County Fairground Lakes Mann Lake

**Location:** Adams County Regional Park. 9755 Henderson Road. 1 mile west of US 85 on 124th Avenue. Parking area north side of lake.
**Size:** 50 acres.
**Fish:** Crappie, largemouth bass, catfish, bluegill, carp.
**Agency:** Adams County Parks & Community Resources.
**Comments:** Open 7 a.m. to 11 p.m. Restrooms available, camping in designated sites.

## Public Works Lake

**Location:** Adams County Regional Park. 9755 Henderson Road. 1 mile west of US 85 on 124th Avenue. Parking in campground, handicap accessible.
**Size:** 20 acres.
**Fish:** Crappie, largemouth bass, catfish, bluegill carp.
**Agency:** Adams County Parks & Community Resources.
**Comments:** Open 7 a.m. to 11 p.m. Restrooms available, camping in designated sites, handicap accessible.

## 3 Brighton City Park Lake

**Location:** From highway 85, east on Hwy 7 to 11th Ave., north on 11th Ave. to Baseline Rd. Lake is on the SW corner of 11th and Baseline Rd.
**Size:** 2.4 acres; maximum depth 16 feet.
**Fish:** Largemouth bass, bluegill, crappie, yellow perch, channel catfish, and catchable trout. (In Spring.)
**Agency:** City of Brighton.
**Comments:** Handicapped accessible fishing pier. No Boats. Fish habitat improvements in pond.

## 4 Grandview Ponds

**Location:** Adams County - Off 104th and Riverdale Rd.
**Size:** 4 ponds; 10 acres total; 8 feet maximum depth.
**Agency:** Colorado Division of Wildlife.
**Fish:** Largemouth bass, bluegill, channel catfish, crappie, bullhead, green sunfish, and yellow perch.
**Special Regulations:** All largemouth bass and smallmouth bass taken must be 15 inches or longer.
**Comments:** Parking area off 104th Ave.

## 5 Hunter's Glen Lake

**Location:** Northeast of the intersection of 128th and Washington. Parking area access from 128th.
**Size:** 19.8 acres; 5 feet maximum depth (3 feet average).
**Fish:** Largemouth bass, bluegill, green sunfish, crappie and channel catfish.
**Agency:** Thornton Department of Parks & Recreation.
**Comments:** Belly boats allowed.

## 5a Loc Amora Pond (Jacob's Pond)

**Location:** From intersection of Hwy 287 and Interstate 36, go north through Broomfield on Hwy 287. Turn west on Miramonte Blvd. and follow to Loc Amora Park, pond is located on south side of park.
**Size:** 3.0 acres; 8 feet maximum depth.
**Fish:** Largemouth bass, bluegill, pumpkinseed sunfish, black bullhead, and channel catfish.
**Agency:** Broomfield Parks and Recreation Department.
**Comments:** No boats. Handicapped accessible fishing pier accessed off of Rock Creek Rd.

## 6 Broomfield Community Park Ponds

**Location:** East of Hwy 287 (Quartz Street), via Midway Blvd. Parking by east pond at Main Street and Community Park Drive.
**Size:** 2 ponds; 3 acres total; 6 feet maximum depth.
**Fish:** Largemouth bass, bluegill, bullhead, channel catfish, green sunfish, and yellow perch.
**Agency:** Broomfield Parks & Recreation.
**Comments:** Open 5 a.m. to 11 p.m. No boats. Playground and restrooms.

# Section 1 - Map 2

## 7 Webster Lake

**Location:** Entrance on E. 117th Ave. west of Washington Street. Parking area on 117th.
**Size:** 13 acres; 12 feet maximum depth.
**Fish:** Bluegill, bullhead, channel catfish, crappie, largemouth bass, yellow perch and rainbow trout (catchable size stocked).
**Agency:** Northglenn Parks & Recreation.
**Comments:** Open 5 a.m. to 11p.m. No boats. Handicapped accessible fishing pier on the south shore. Playground and restrooms. Extreme water level fluctuation. Hard surface foot trail.

## 8 Croke Reservoir (Carlson Reservoir)

**Location:** North of 104th and Huron St.

Fishing Pier at Webster Lake

**Size:** 16 acres; 10 feet maximum depth.
**Fish:** Largemouth bass, pumpkinseed sunfish, bluegill, green sunfish and black bullhead.
**Agency:** Northglenn Parks & Recreation.
**Special Regulations:** All largemouth and smallmouth bass taken must be 15 inches or larger. Fishing by artificial flies or lures only. No boats or tubing.
**Comments:** Fishing allowed from April 1 thru Oct. 15. Open 5 a.m. to 11 p.m. north shore closed to fishing.

## 8a Community College Pond

**Location:** From intersection of 112th Ave. and Sheridan Blvd., go east on 112th. Park in farthest west parking lot of Front Range Community College. Take foot-trail along path north to lake.
**Size:** 2.4 acres; 12 feet maximum depth.
**Fish:** Largemouth bass, bluegill, yellow perch, crappie and channel catfish.
**Agency:** Westminster Parks and Recreation Department.
**Comments:** Underwater artificial fish habitat structures (tree bundles, Christmas trees, etc.) placed in lake during construction. Lake is handicapped accessible from the Big Dry Creek recreation trail. No Boats.

## 8b Westminster City Park Pond

**Location:** At 104th Ave. and Sheridan Blvd., go north on Sheridan, take first left into Westminster Recreation Facility entrance. Then take first right and follow service road around north side of soccer fields, the lake sits northwest of the recreation center.
**Size:** 7.4 acres; 14 feet maximum depth.
**Fish:** Largemouth bass, bluegill, yellow perch, crappie and rainbow trout (catchable size in spring).
**Agency:** Westminster Parks and Recreation Department.
**Comments:** Foot-trail around entire lake, handicapped accessible from cement pavilion area on east side, surrounding picnic areas. No boats. Fish habitat improvements in pond.

## 8c Water Point and Bellio Ponds (Hyland Ponds)

**Location:** Turn west onto 100th Ave. from Sheridan Blvd. parking available along street. Walk-in access from foot-trails.
**Size:** Two lakes: 2.5 acres each; 14 feet maximum depth.
**Fish:** Largemouth bass, bluegill, green sunfish and channel catfish.
**Agency:** Westminster Parks and Recreation Department.

Standley Lake boat ramp

**Comments:** No boats. Handicapped accessible fishing piers. Fish habitat improvements in ponds.

## 9 Ketner Lake

**Location:** Off west 100th Ave. and County Side Drive.
**Size:** 25 acres; 30 feet maximum depth.
**Fish:** Largemouth bass, crappie, bluegill, green sunfish, yellow perch and bullhead.
**Agency:** City of Westminster.
**Comments:** Belly boats allowed for fishing. Ice fishing prohibited.
**Special Regulations:** All largemouth and smallmouth bass taken must be 15 inches or longer.

## 10 Standley Lake

**Location:** W. 88th Ave. and Kipling Street. Parking area is off Kipling. West side of the lake - Eagle nest area, fishing restricted.
**Size:** 1,210 acres; 80 feet maximum depth.
**Fish:** Bluegill, carp, channel catfish, green sunfish, largemouth bass, smallmouth bass, sucker, walleye, yellow perch, wiper and rainbow trout (catchable size stocked).
**Agency:** South and southwest shore, Jefferson County Open Space. Remaining shore and lake itself, City of Westminster Parks & Recreation.
**Comments:** Hours as posted, walk-in only spring and fall. All boats over 20 h.p. need Westminster boat permit. Fee area for vehicles at Kipling & W. 88th Ave. Walk-in fishing free. Extreme water fluctuation. Boat ramp on east shore and north shore (dirt boat ramp).No fishing from dam.
**Special Regulations:** All wipers taken must be 15 inches or longer.

## 11 Pomona Lake

**Location:** In Meadow Glen Park. North of W. 80th Ave. and one-quarter mile west of Wadsworth Blvd. Main parking area can be reached via 80th Ave. by going north on Club Crest Drive, and east on W. 81st Place.
**Size:** 31 acres; 8 feet maximum depth.
**Fish:** Largemouth bass, yellow perch, bullhead, channel catfish, crappie and green sunfish.
**Agency:** North Jeffco Parks & Recreation.
**Comments:** Open dawn to 11 p.m. No boats. Paved trail.

## 12 Lake Arbor

**Location:** North of W. 80th Ave. off Pomona Drive or Lamar Street between Wadsworth Blvd. and Sheridan Blvd.
**Size:** 37 acres; 19 feet maximum depth.
**Fish:** Bluegill, bullhead, carp, channel catfish, crappie, green sunfish, largemouth bass, pumpkinseed sunfish and sucker. Grass carp stocked to control aquatic plants.
**Agency:** North Jeffco Parks & Recreation and City of Arvada.
**Comments:** Open dawn to 11 p.m. Non-motorized boats only. Fishing piers located on the north shore. Artificial fish habitat structures in lake. Playground. Hard surface foot trail.
**Special Regulations:** All Largemouth and Smallmouth Bass taken must be 15 inches or longer. Bag and possession limits for walleye is 5 fish, 15 inches or longer.

## 13 Faversham Park Pond

**Location:** Depew and 73rd Ave., NW off 72nd Ave.
**Size:** 6 acres; 11 feet maximum depth.
**Fish:** Bluegill.
**Agency:** Westminster Parks & Recreation.
**Comments:** Open sunrise to 11 p.m. No boats. No wading

or swimming. Kids 15 years old and under are allowed to fish.

### 14 Camenisch Park Pond

**Location:** West of Pecos Street, south of W. 90th Ave. at Fontaine Street. Parking area south of 90th Ave.
**Size:** 3 acres; 10 feet maximum depth.
**Fish:** Largemouth bass, pumpkinseed sunfish, sucker, bluegill, bullhead, channel catfish, crappie and green sunfish.
**Agency:** Hyland Hills Recreation & Park District.
**Comments:** Open dawn to 10 p.m. No boats. Playground and restrooms. Hard surface foot trail.

### 15 Bell Roth Park Pond

**Location:** On the east side of Pecos Street, 2 blocks north of W. 84th Ave.
**Size:** 3 acres; 8 feet maximum depth.
**Fish:** Channel catfish, crappie, green sunfish, sucker, yellow perch, bluegill, bullhead and carp.
**Agency:** Hyland Hills Recreation & Park District.
**Comments:** Open dawn to 10 p.m. No boats. Playground.

### 16 Kiwanis Park Pond

**Location:** W. 80th Ave. east of Zuni Street. Parking area south of 80th Ave.
**Size:** 3 acres; 2 feet maximum depth.
**Fish:** Bullhead and green sunfish.
**Agency:** Hyland Hills Recreation & Park District.
**Comments:** Open dawn to half hour after sunset. No boats.

### 17 Rotella Park Pond

**Location:** North of E. 78th Ave. between N. Washington Street and N. York Street. Parking north of 78th Ave. or south of Coronado Drive So.
**Size:** 3 acres; 10 feet maximum depth.
**Fish:** Bluegill, bullhead, largemouth bass, channel catfish and pumpkinseed sunfish.
**Agency:** Adams County Park & Recreation.
**Comments:** Open dawn to dusk. No boats. Extreme water level fluctuation. Playground and restrooms. Hard surface foot trail.

### 18 Engineers Lake

**Location:** From I-76 go to Hwy 224. Travel west on Hwy 224. Parking area is south of Hwy 224, just west of the South Platte River. The lake is at the confluence of Clear Creek and the South Platte River. Hard surface foot trail across the river.
**Size:** 1 acre; 25 feet maximum depth.
**Fish:** Bullhead.
**Agency:** Adams County Parks & Recreation.
**Comments:** Open dawn to dusk. No boats. Walk-in trail and steep shoreline. Picnic shelter.

### 19 Clear Creek Pond

**Location:** South of Hwy 224 between Washington Street and York Street. Parking area is south of Hwy 224 and east of Washington Street.
**Size:** 3 acres; 9 feet maximum depth.
**Fish:** Bluegill, bullhead, carp, channel catfish, crappie, pumpkinseed sunfish, green sunfish, largemouth bass and yellow perch.
**Agency:** Adams County Parks & Recreation.
**Comments:** Open dawn to dusk. No boats. Hard surface trail along side of pond.

### 20 Twin Lakes Park Ponds

**Location:** Just west of Broadway on 70th Ave. Parking area south from 70th Ave.
**Size:** 2 ponds; 7 acres total; 16 feet maximum depth.
**Fish:** Bullhead, carp, channel catfish, crappie, green sunfish, largemouth bass, sucker and yellow perch.
**Agency:** Adams County Parks & Recreation.
**Comments:** Open dawn to dusk. No boats. Hard surface foot trail which connects with Clear Creek Trail.

**Arvada/Blunn Reservoir pier**

### 21 Arvada Reservoir

**Location:** Between Hwy 93 and Indiana on W 66th Ave.
**Size:** 180 acres; 77 feet maximum depth.
**Fish:** Rainbow trout (catchable-size stocked), tiger muskie, walleye, largemouth bass, smallmouth bass, yellow perch.
**Agency:** City of Arvada.
**Comments:** Arvada permit required; available at Arvada City Hall - Daily passes sold at gate. No ice fishing. Non-motorized boats only. Open sunrise to sunset. Hard surface foot trail.
**Special Regulations:** Two trout bag limit. ♿

### 21a Sprat Platte Lake

**Location:** From 1-76, west on 96th Ave to McKay Rd. North to 100th Ave. then west. Parking off 100th Ave.
**Size:** 60 acres; 23 feet maximum depth.
**Fish:** Largemouth bass, bluegill, yellow perch, green sunfish, crappie, black bullhead, chanel catfish and carp.
**Agency:** Colorado Division of Wildlife
**Comments:** Handicap accessible pier and restrooms. Picnic shelters and hard surface trails.
**Special Regulations:** 18-inch minimum size limit on largemouth bass. Flies and lures only. No watercraft.

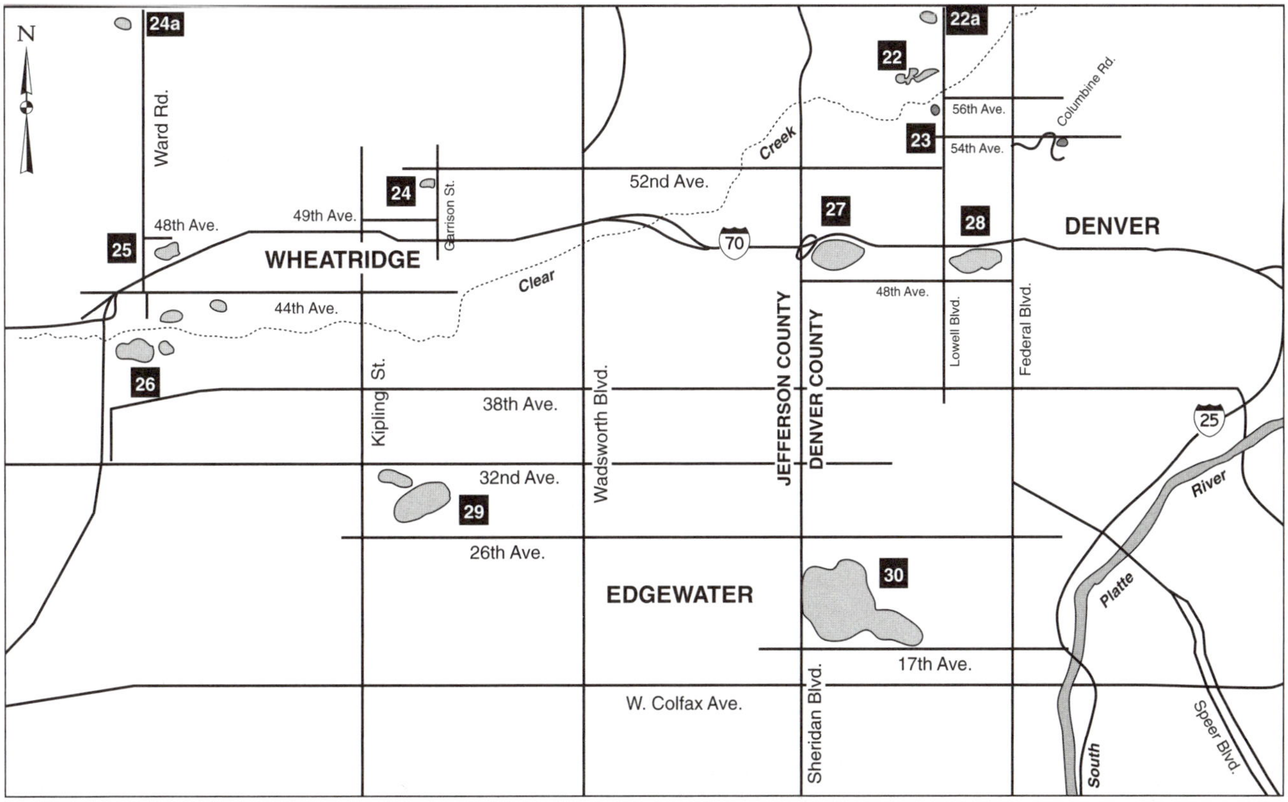

SECTION 1 - MAP 3

## 22 Lowell Ponds

**Location:** Adams County, West of Lowell Street on 56th Way.
**Size:** 3 ponds; 11,2 and 2 acres. Plus Sheets Lake, 5 acres. (Leased from City of Westminster.) Maximum Depth 10 ft.
**Fish:** Largemouth bass, smallmouth bass, channel catfish, bluegill, crappie and bullhead.
**Agency:** Colorado Division of Wildlife.
**Comments:** Belly boats allowed for fishing, except on Sheets Lake. Handicapped accessible fishing pier. Artificial fish habitat structures in ponds.
**Special Regulation:** All largemouth and smallmouth bass taken must be 15 inches or longer.

## 22a Jim Baker Reservoir

**Location:** South of 64th Ave. and Lowell Blvd. intersection on West side of Lowell. Parking area at South-West corner of reservoir, access off of Tennyson St. from 64th Ave.
**Size:** 80 acres; 30 feet maximum depth.
**Fish:** Rainbow trout (catchable-size stocked), smallmouth bass, yellow perch, walleye, bluegill and crappie.
**Agency:** Adams County Parks and Recreation Department.
**Comments:** Walk-in access along foot trails. No boats.

## 23 Carl Park Pond

**Location:** West of Federal Blvd., on W. 54th Ave. at Meade Street. Parking area north of 54th Ave.
**Size:** 4 acres; 8 feet maximum depth.
**Fish:** Largemouth bass, bluegill and bullhead.
**Agency:** Hyland Hills Recreation & Park District.
**Comments:** Open dawn to 10 p.m. No boats.

## 24 Birdland Lake (Jack B. Tomlinson Park)

**Location:** W 51st Ave. and Garrison Street. Parking area west of Garrison at south end of lake.
**Size:** 3 acres; 10 feet maximum depth.
**Fish:** Bluegill, channel catfish, green sunfish, largemouth bass, pumpkinseed sunfish and yellow perch.
**Agency:** North Jeffco Recreation & Park District.
**Comments:** Open dawn to 11 p.m. Non-motorized boats only. No ice fishing. Playground and hard surface trail.

## 24a Meadow Park Lake

**Location:** West of intersection of Ward Rd. and W. 64th Ave. Turn south on Yank Way from 64th Ave., then right to Yank Ct.
**Size:** 5 acres; 8 feet maximum depth.
**Fish:** Largemouth bass, bluegill, pumpkinseed sunfish, crappie, yellow perch, black bullhead and common carp.
**Agency:** City of Arvada.
**Comments:** No boats.

## 25 Ward Road Pond

**Location:** Northeast of the intersection of I-70 and Ward Road. Parking area east of Ward Road and South of W. 48th Ave.
**Size:** 7 acres; 30 feet maximum depth.

**Fish:** Largemouth bass, pumpkinseed sunfish, bluegill, bullhead, crappie and green sunfish.
**Agency:** City of Arvada and Colorado Division of Wildlife.
**Comments:** Non-motorized boats only. Belly boats allowed. Pond open for fishing only. Good bass fishing. Restroom. Artificial fish habitat structures in pond.
**Special Regulations:** 1. Fishing by artificial flies or artificial lures only; 2. All fish caught must be returned to water immediately.

Prospect Park Lake

## 26 Prospect Park Lakes

**Location:** East of I-70 and south of W. 44th Ave. Parking for Prospect Lake and North Prospect Lake is available south on 44th on Robb Street, next to park headquarters. Parking for West Lake and Bass Lake is available south of 44th on Youngfield Street. Foot trail runs between all the lakes along Clear Creek.
**Size:** Bass Lake: 3 acres; 13 feet maximum depth.
North Prospect: 16 acres; 26 feet maximum depth.
Prospect Lake: 7 acres; 22 feet maximum depth.
West Lake: 46 acres; 15 feet maximum depth.
**Fish:** Bass Lake: Largemouth bass, bluegill, crappie, green sunfish, and sucker.
North Prospect: (Tabor): Largemouth bass, bluegill, channel catfish, crappie and green sunfish. Artificial fish habitat structures in lake.
Prospect Lake: Largemouth bass, bluegill, channel, catfish, crappie and green sunfish.
West Lake: Largemouth bass, pumpkinseed sunfish, sucker, bluegill, bullhead, crappie and green sunfish. Artificial fish habitat structures in lake.
**Agency:** Wheat Ridge Parks & Recreation.
**Comments:** Open dawn to dusk except for Prospect Lake, which is open until 10 p.m. No boats on Bass Lake. Non-motorized boats allowed on other lakes with a Wheat Ridge Parks Permit. Prospect Lake has a boat ramp and restrooms. Good bass fishing. Some steep banks. Hard surface trail along Clear Creek.
**Special Regulations:** 1. All smallmouth and largemouth bass taken must be 15 inches in length or longer; 2. Bass Lake and West Prospect Lake (south of Clear Creek) - fishing by artificial flies or artificial lures only.

## 27 Berkeley Lake

**Location:** South of I-70 between Sheridan Blvd. and Tennyson Street. Main entrance is on 46th Ave. with parking. Also access from Tennyson Street.
**Size:** 40 acres; 12 feet maximum depth.
**Fish:** Largemouth bass, orange spotted sunfish, sucker, green sunfish, bluegill, bullhead, carp, channel catfish, crappie and rainbow trout (catchable size stocked in spring).
**Agency:** Denver Parks & Recreation.
**Comments:** Open 5 a.m. to 11 p.m. No boats. Recreation center, Playground and restrooms on the south side of lake.

## 28 Rocky Mountain Lake

**Location:** W. 46th Ave. between Federal Blvd. and Lowell Blvd. Parking areas north of 46th Ave.
**Size:** 29 acres; 14 feet maximum depth.
**Fish:** Rainbow trout (catchable size stocked in spring), bluegill, bullhead, carp, channel catfish, crappie, green sunfish, largemouth bass, pumpkinseed sunfish, sucker.
**Agency:** Denver Parks & Recreation.
**Comments:** Open 5 a.m. to 11 p.m. No boats. Playground and restrooms. Hard surface foot trail.

## 29 Crown Hill Lake

**Location:** Northeast of the intersection of Kipling Street and W. 26th Ave. Parking access is north of 26th Ave. with two parking areas. Hard surface foot trail and bridle path access also from Kipling.
**Size:** 53 acres; 13 feet maximum depth.
**Fish:** Largemouth bass, bluegill, sucker, carp, channel catfish, crappie, green sunfish and yellow perch.
**Agency:** Jeffco Open Space.
**Comments:** Open one hour prior to dawn, closed one hour past dusk. Restrooms on 26th Ave. side of lake. No boats. Playground. Several artificial fish habitat structures in the lake. No wading or float tubes. Handicapped fishing pier north of parking lot. Wildlife sanctuary.

## 30 Sloan Lake

**Location:** East of Sheridan Blvd. between W. 25th Ave. and W 17th Ave. Parking area all around lake.
**Size:** 174 acres; 9 feet maximum depth.
**Fish:** Bluegill, bullhead, carp, channel catfish, crappie, green sunfish, orange spotted sunfish, rainbow trout (catchable-size stocked in spring), sucker and yellow perch.
**Agency:** Denver Parks and Recreation.
**Comments:** Boating with permit. No fishing from boats. Premier carp fishery. Boat house and boat ramp. Playground and restrooms. Hard surface foot trail around lake.

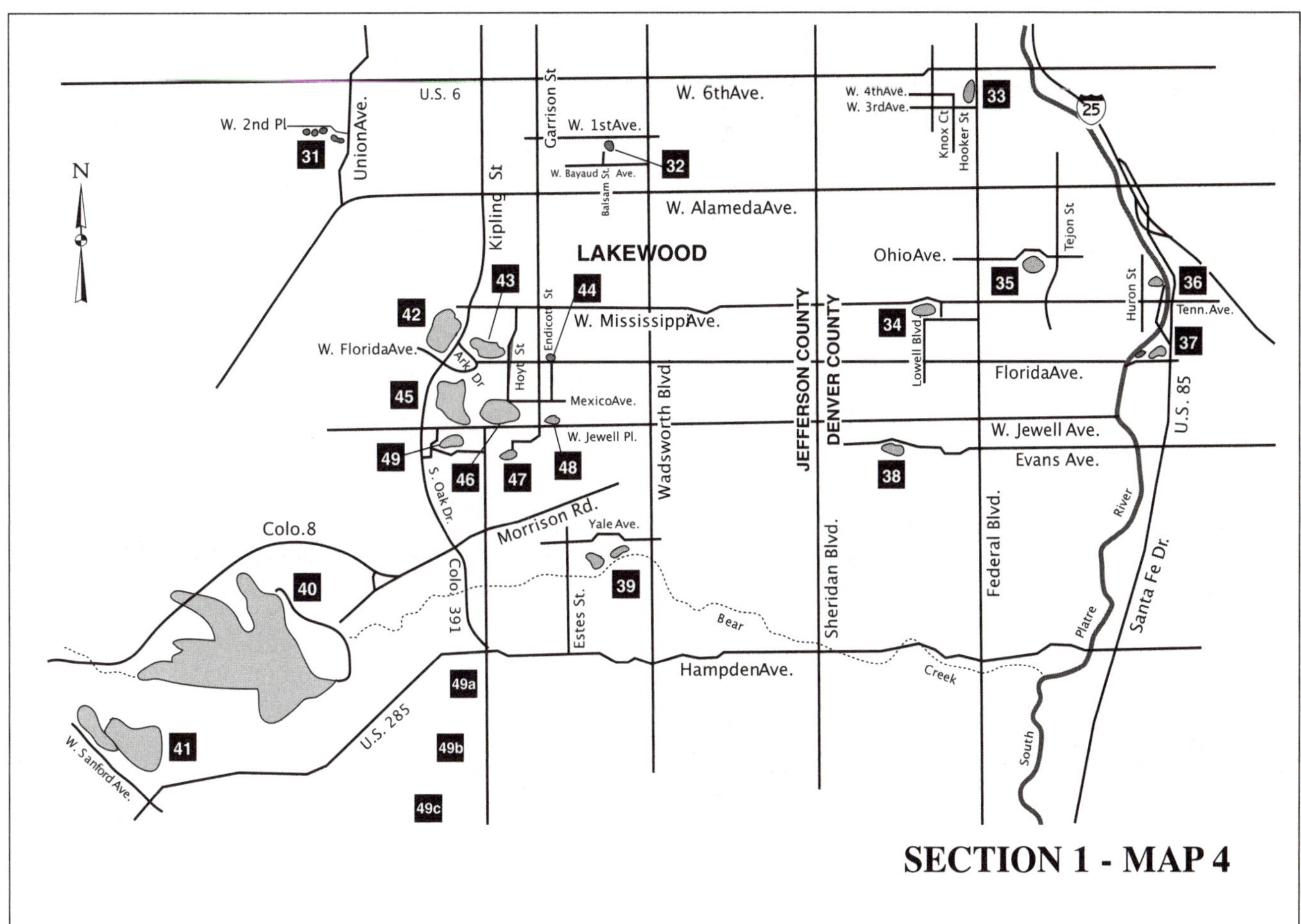


## 31 Union Square Ponds

**Location:** South of W. 6th Ave. and West of S. Union St. Access via W. 2nd Place and S. VanGordon St. The ponds are just west of the Denver Federal Center.
**Size:** 5 ponds; 8 acres total; 8 feet maximum depth.
**Fish:** Bluegill, carp, channel catfish, green sunfish and largemouth bass.
**Agency:** Union Square Development Co. and Lakewood Parks and Recreation.
**Comments:** No boats.

## 32 Balsam Park Pond

**Location:** West of S Wadsworth, south Of W. 1st Ave. at Balsam St.
**Size:** 1.5 acres; 6 feet maximum depth.
**Fish:** Bluegill, bullhead, carp, crappie, green sunfish, and sucker.
**Agency:** Lakewood Department of Community Resources.
**Comments:** Open dawn to 10:30 p.m. No boats.

## 33 Barnum Park Lake

**Location:** West of Federal Blvd. between 6th Ave. and 3rd Ave., with parking access from Hooker St.
**Size:** 9 acres; 5 feet maximum depth.
**Fish:** Bluegill, carp, channel catfish and sucker.
**Agency:** Denver Parks and Recreation.
**Comments:** Open 5 a.m. to 11 p.m. No boats. Playground, restrooms and recreation center.

## 34 Garfield Lake

**Location:** South of W. Mississippi Ave. between S. Federal Blvd. and S. Sheridan Blvd. Access from either S. Lowell Blvd. and Mississippi, or S. Newton St. and W. Arizona (east from S. Osceola St.).
**Size:** 10 acres; 4 feet maximum depth.
**Fish:** Largemouth bass, bluegill, carp, channel catfish, crappie, and green sunfish.
**Agency:** Denver Parks and Recreation.
**Comments:** Open 5 a.m. to 11 p.m. No boats. Recreation Center, playground and restrooms.

## 35 Huston Park Lake

**Location:** East of S. Federal Blvd. about 4 blocks, between W. Ohio Ave. and W. Kentucky Ave. Southeast of the intersection of Ohio and S. Clay St.
**Size:** 13 acres; 6 feet maximum depth.
**Fish:** Largemouth bass, sucker, yellow perch, green sunfish, bluegill, bullhead, carp, channel catfish, and crappie.
**Agency:** Denver Parks and Recreation.
**Comments:** Open 5 a.m. to 11 p.m. No boats, Recreation Center, playground and restrooms. Hard surface foot trail around lake.

## 36 Vanderbilt Park Pond

**Location:** North of W. Tennessee Ave. between S. Santa Fe Drive and S. Huron St. in Vanderbilt Park. Access

Fishing Bear Creek Reservoir

Yurt available for rent at Bear Creek Lake Park

from W. Mississippi Ave.
**Size:** 6 acres; 15 feet maximum depth.
**Fish:** Green sunfish.
**Agency:** Denver Parks and Recreation.
**Comments:** Open 5 a.m. to 11 p.m. No boats. Hard surface foot trail.

## 37 Overland Park Pond

**Location:** North of W. Florida Ave. between S. Santa Fe Dr. and South Platte River Trail. Parking area is north of Florida.
**Size:** 1 acre; 7 feet maximum depth.
**Fish:** Bluegill, carp, largemouth bass, bullhead and crappie.
**Agency:** Denver Parks and Recreation.
**Comments:** Open 5 a.m. to 11 p.m. No boats. Fly casting practice pad on south shore. Hard surface foot trail.

## 38 Harvey Park Lake

**Location:** Between S Sheridan Blvd. and S. Federal. Just south of W. Evans Ave. and east of S. Tennyson St. Hard surface foot trail across from Evans.
**Size:** 8.5 acres; 14 feet maximum depth.
**Fish:** Bluegill, bullhead, carp, channel catfish, crappie, green sunfish, largemouth bass pumpkinseed sunfish, and yellow perch.
**Agency:** Denver Parks and Recreation.
**Comments:** Open 5 a.m. to 11 p.m. No boats. Recreation Center. Playground and restrooms.

## 39 Bear Creek Ponds

**Location:** West of S Wadsworth and south of Yale Ave. on the east side of S. Estes St. Parking on Estes Street.
**Size:** 10 acres total; 12 feet maximum depth.
**Fish:** Bluegill, bullhead, channel catfish, crappie, green sunfish, and largemouth bass.
**Agency:** Lakewood Department of Community Resources.
**Comments:** Open 6 a.m. to 10 p.m. No boats. Fishing pier on the west side of the west pond.

## 40 Bear Creek Reservoir

**Location:** South of Morrison Rd. (Hwy 8), north of W. Hampden Ave. (US 285), west of S. Kipling St., and east of C-470. The main entrance to the park is on Morrison Rd., with several parking areas on the north side of the reservoir.
**Size:** 110 acres; 36 feet maximum depth.
**Fish:** Largemouth bass, smallmouth bass, bluegill, green sunfish, bullhead, rainbow trout, (catchable-size stocked), sucker, tiger muskie, and yellow perch.
**Agency:** Lakewood Department of Community Resources.
**Comments:** Open 7 a.m. to 8 p.m. from May to September. Open 7 a.m. to 8 p.m. in October and April. Open 8 a.m. to 6 p.m. from November to March. Boats to 10 hp at wakeless speeds. Boat ramp and picnic shelter on the north side of the reservoir. Fee area $3.00 per car, free walk in access. Ice fishing allowed as posted.
**Special Regulations:** Tiger muskie; one fish only, 30 inches or longer.

## 41 Soda Lakes

**Location:** South of Morrison Road (Hwy 8), north of W. Hampden Ave. (US 285), west of S. Kipling Street, and east of C 4-70. The main entrance to the park is on Morrison Road, with several parking areas on the north side of the reservoir. Also an entrance on Soda Lakes Road, for park and walk access.

Big Soda Lake in Bear Creek Lake Park

**Size:** Big Soda (South) - 96 acres.
Little Soda (North) - 44 acres. 40 feet maximum depth.
**Fish:** Yellow perch, largemouth and smallmouth bass, channel catfish, green sunfish and sucker.
**Agency:** Lakewood Department of Community Resources.
**Comments:** Non-motorized boat rental area on Big Soda.

## 42 Main Reservoir (Osner Reservoir)

**Location:** West of S. Kipling Street between W. Mississippi Ave. and W. Florida Ave.
**Size:** 45 acres; 19 feet maximum depth.
**Fish:** Bluegill, carp, channel catfish, crappie, green sunfish, largemouth bass, pumpkinseed sunfish, rainbow trout (catchable size stocked in spring), smallmouth bass, sucker and yellow perch.
**Agency:** Lakewood Department of Community Resources.
**Comments:** Open 6:00 a.m. to 10:00. No boats. Extreme water level fluctuation.

## 43 East Reservoir

**Location:** East of Kipling Street between W. Florida Ave. and W. Mississippi Ave. Access from W. Florida via W. Arkansas Drive.
**Size:** 21 acres; 5 feet maximum depth.
**Fish:** Bullhead, carp, green sunfish, largemouth bass pumpkinseed sunfish and yellow perch.
**Agency:** Lakewood Department of Community Resources.
**Comments:** Open 5 a.m. to 10 p.m.. No boats. Extreme water level fluctuation.

## 44 Green Gables Park Pond

**Location:** 1450 Garrison Street. Six blocks north of Jewell on Garrison Street. Parking off Garrison. Hard surface trail around pond.

**Size:** 0.5 acres; 6 feet maximum depth.
**Fish:** Bluegill, crappie, green sunfish, largemouth bass and pumpkinseed sunfish.
**Agency:** Foothills Park Metro. & Recreation District.
**Comments:** Open 5 a.m. to 10 p.m. No boats, wading or flotation devices.

## 45 Smith Reservoir

**Location:** East of S. Kipling Street, north of Jewell Ave. Parking area east of S. Moore Court.
**Size:** 44 acres; 17 feet maximum depth.
**Fish:** Bluegill, carp, channel catfish, crappie, green sunfish, largemouth bass, pumpkinseed sunfish, smallmouth bass, sucker and yellow perch.
**Agency:** Lakewood Department of Community Resources.
**Comments:** Open 5:00 a.m. to 11:00 p.m. No boats. Extreme water level fluctuation. Two previous state record smallmouth bass caught here.

## 46 Kendrick Park Reservoir

**Location:** 9500 W. Jewell Ave. 9 blocks west of Wadsworth on the north side of Jewell. Playground and trail access off South Hoyt Street.
**Size:** 33 acres; 8 feet maximum depth.
**Fish:** Bluegill, bullhead, carp, channel catfish, crappie, largemouth bass, pumpkinseed sunfish and yellow perch.
**Agency:** Foothills Metro. Parks & Recreation District.
**Comments:** Open dawn to 10:00 p.m. No boats, wading or flotation devices. Fishing pier on southwest shore.

## 47 Jewell Park Pond

**Location:** North of W. Jewell Ave. between S. Garrison Street and S. Wadsworth Blvd. Access from S. Dover Way.
**Size:** 2 acres; 5 feet maximum depth.
**Fish:** Bluegill, bullhead, carp, channel catfish, crappie, green sunfish and pumpkinseed sunfish.
**Agency:** Lakewood Department of Community Resources.
**Comments:** Open dawn to 10:30 p.m. Non-motorized boats only. Fishing pier on the south shore. Hard Surface foot trail.

## 48 Cottonwood Park Lake

**Location:** From the Kipling Parkway and W. Jewell Ave., go east on Jewell to S. Oak Street. Then 1 block south on Oak to Park. On Street parking on Oak St. Lake and hard surface trails 75 yards east of Oak St.
**Size:** 8 acres; 14 feet maximum depth.
**Fish:** Bluegill, channel catfish, largemouth bass, pumpkinseed sunfish and yellow perch.
**Agency:** Foothills Metro. Parks & Recreation District.
**Comments:** Open 5:00 a.m. to 10:00 p.m. No boats, wading or floatation devices.

## 49 Carmody Park Pond

**Location:** 2200 South Old Kipling Street. From Kipling Parkway and Jewell head east on Jewell to old Kipling Street. 50 yards east of swimming complex.
**Size:** .25 acres; 4 feet maximum depth.
**Fish:** Bluegill, bullhead and largemouth bass.
**Agency:** Foothills Metro. Park & Recreation District.
**Comments:** Open 5 a.m. to 10 p.m. No boats, wading or floatation devices.

## 49a Harriman Lake Reservoir

**Location:** W. Quincy Ave. and S. Kipling Parkway. Parking off Kipling. Trail to lake.
**Size:** 70 acres; 18 feet maximum depth.
**Fish:** Bluegill, green catfish, largemouth bass, crappie, common carp and white sucker.
**Agency:** Foothills Metro. Park & Recreation District.
**Comments:** Open 5 a.m. to 10 p.m. No boats, wading or floatation devices.

## 49b Hine Lake Reservoir

**Location:** From west Coalmine Road and South Simms Street Head West on Coalmine Road 1/4 mile to S. Van Gordon. Street. Park in ridge at West Meadow Park parking lot. Hard surface foot trail around half the lake.
**Size:** 50 acres; 15 feet maximum depth.

**Pier at Hine Lake**

**Fish:** Bluegill, largemouth bass, pumpkinseed sunfish, green sunfish and hybrid bluegill.
**Agency:** Foothills Metro. Park & Recreation District.
**Comments:** Open 5 a.m. to 10 p.m. No boats, wading or floatation devices. Playground and picnic area.

## 49c Blue Heron Lake

**Location:** Go north on S. Simms St. from intersection of W. Bowles Ave. and S. Simms St. turn right on W. Brandt Place follow to T-intersection at S. Quail St. Parking allowed along street.
**Size:** 8 acres; 12 feet maximum depth.
**Fish:** Largemouth bass, bluegill, crappie, green sunfish, black bullhead and fathead minnow.
**Agency:** Foothills Metro. Park and Recreation Department.
**Comments:** Playground and foot trail around lake. No boats.

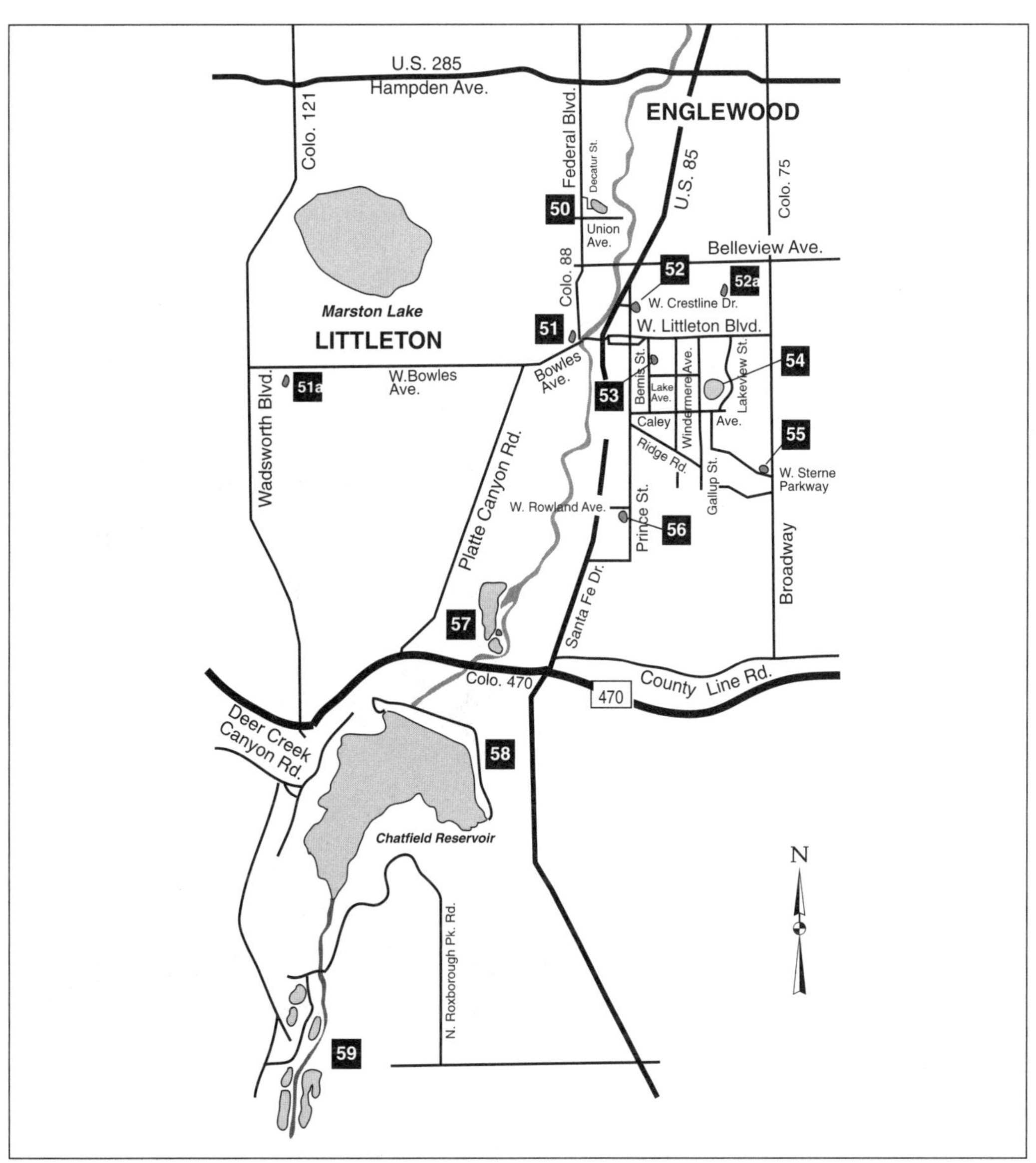


SECTION 1 - MAP 5

## 50 Centennial Park Lake

**Location:** From the intersection of W. Union Ave. and S. Federal Blvd., go north on Federal to Stanford Ave. Turn east on Stanford to S. Decatur Street. Parking area is on the northeast corner of the intersection of Decatur and Stanford. There is a parking area further south of Decatur past the softball field.
**Size:** 15 acres; 27 feet maximum depth.
**Fish:** Largemouth and smallmouth bass, pumpkinseed sunfish, rainbow trout (catchable-size stocked), yellow perch, bluegill, channel catfish, sucker, crappie and green sunfish.
**Agency:** Englewood Parks & Recreation.
**Comments:** Open dawn to 11 p.m. No boats. Playground and restrooms. Handicapped accessible fishing pier on the west side of the lake. Hard surface foot trail to the pier. Artificial fish habitat structures in lake.

## 51 Bowles Grove Pond

**Location:** Northwest of the intersection of S. Federal Blvd. and W. Bowles Ave. Parking west of Federal at north end of the lake.
**Size:** 2 acres; 6 feet maximum depth.
**Fish:** Largemouth bass, bluegill, bullhead, carp, crappie, green sunfish, orange spotted sunfish, sucker and yellow perch.
**Agency:** South Suburban Recreation & Park District.
**Comments:** Open 6 a.m. to 10 p.m. No boats hard surface foot trail.

## 51a Johnston Reservoir (Clement Park)

**Location:** At the corner of W. Bowles Ave. and S. Wadsworth Blvd. Parking available in Clement Park, directly east of lake.
**Size:** 58.5 acres; 12 feet maximum depth.
**Fish:** Largemouth bass, bluegill, yellow perch, crappie, smallmouth bass, common carp and some rainbow trout privately stocked from fishing clinic events.
**Agency:** Foothills Parks and Recreation Department, Jefferson County Open Space.
**Comments:** Hard surface foot-trail around lake perimeter, cement pavilion areas and no boats.

## 52 Lake Geneva

**Location:** South of Crestline Ave. between S. Prince Street and S. Windermere Street. South of the Arapaho County Administration Building.
**Size:** 1 acre; 12 feet maximum depth.
**Fish:** Bluegill, crappie, green sunfish, bullhead, carp, channel catfish, sucker and largemouth bass.
**Agency:** City of Littleton.
**Comments:** No boats. Fishing is for Handicapped persons, senior citizens only and kids under 15 only.

## 52a Progress Park Pond

**Location:** Go east on E. Belleview Ave. from intersection of S. Santa Fe and E. Belleview Ave. Turn south on Hickory St. some parking available along Hickory. Progress Park is immediately southeast of Belleview and Hickory.
**Size:** 1.0 acres; 10 feet maximum depth.
**Fish:** Largemouth bass, bluegill, green sunfish, pumpkinseed, yellow perch, black bullhead and channel catfish.
**Agency:** South Suburban Parks and Recreation District.
**Comments:** Wetland theme playground nearby, Little Dry Creek trail access and handicapped accessible fishing pier. No boats.

## 53 Sterne Pond

**Location:** From the intersection of Littleton Blvd. and S. Bemis Street go south on Bemis. Turn east at W. Aberdeen Ave. At S. Spotswood Street go south to parking area.
**Size:** 3 acres; 3 feet maximum depth.
**Fish:** Bluegill, crappie, largemouth bass and yellow perch.
**Agency:** South Suburban Recreation & Park District.
**Comments:** Open 6 a.m. to 10 p.m. No boats. Children under 15 years only, are allowed to fish.

Johnston Reservoir

## 54 Ketring Park Lake (Gallup Lake)

**Location:** West of S. Broadway. From the intersection of Littleton Blvd. and S. Gallup Street, travel south on Gallup to W. Shepperd Ave. Turn east on Shepperd to S. Lakeview Street. Go south on Lakeview to the parking area. Access also from Caley Ave. south of the lake, to Lakeview Street and then north to the parking area.
**Size:** 15 acres; 9 feet maximum depth.
**Fish:** Bluegill, carp, channel catfish, crappie, green sunfish and largemouth bass.
**Agency:** South Suburban Recreation & Park District.
**Comments:** Open 6 a.m. to 10 p.m. No boats. Artificial fish habitat structures.

## 55 Little's Creek Pond

**Location:** From the intersection of Arapaho Road and South Broadway, go south on Broadway to Sterne Parkway. Turn west on Sterne Parkway and the lake will be just

Saturday afternoon at Clement Park

north, with access via hard surface foot trail.
**Size:** 1 acre; 5 feet maximum depth.
**Fish:** Bluegill, bullhead, carp, sucker, channel catfish, crappie, green sunfish and largemouth bass.
**Agency:** South Suburban Parks & Recreation District.
**Comments:** Open 6 a.m. to 10 p.m. No boats.

## 56 Ridgeview Park Pond

**Location:** East of Santa Fe Drive and south of Ridge Road. Access from S. Prince Street, S. Costilla Street, W. Rowland, or Houston Warning Circle.
**Size:** 1.5 acres; 6 feet maximum depth.
**Fish:** Largemouth bass, bluegill, carp, channel catfish and green sunfish.
**Agency:** South Suburban Parks & Recreation District.
**Comments:** Open 6 a.m. to 10 p.m. No boats. Picnic tables.

## 57 South Platte Park Ponds (Littleton Flood Plain Ponds)

**Location:** S. Santa Fe Drive and C-470 along South Platte River.
**Size:** 5 ponds; 80 acres total; 27 feet maximum depth.
**Fish:** Bluegill, yellow perch, sucker, rainbow trout and largemouth bass.
**Agency:** City of Littleton and South Suburban Parks & Recreation District.
**Comments:** No boats. Artificial fish habitat structures in some of the ponds. Check with agencies about access. Nature Center.
**Special Regulation:** All smallmouth and largemouth bass taken must be 15 inches in length or longer.

## 58 Chatfield Reservoir State Park

**Location:** In Chatfield Reservoir State Park, between S. Santa Fe Drive (US 85) on the east, and C-470 on the west. From S. Santa Fe go west on County line Road or Titan Road to Roxborough Park Road and go north. Roxborough is the south entrance to the area. From S. Wadsworth go south to C-470 and turn southwest. At Deer Creek Canyon Road turn east, and you will be at the north entrance to the area. There are parking areas all around the reservoir.
**Size:** 1,100 acres; 50 feet maximum depth.
**Fish:** Bluegill, brown trout, bullhead, channel catfish, crappie, green sunfish, largemouth bass, rainbow trout (catchable-size stocked) carp, sucker, walleye and yellow perch.
**Agency:** Colorado State Parks.
**Comments:** Boating, camping, and ice fishing allowed. No boating in heron rookery from March through October. Boat ramps. Extreme water fluctuation possible. Park pass required, free walk-in access for fishermen. Marina. Boat permit required. Swimming area. May close due to capacity. Handicapped accessible fishing piers by the marina and on the river near Kingfisher Cove. Restrooms. Boat rental available. Heron rookery viewing area. Artificial fish habitat structures in lake. (See map at right.) Visitors Center.
**Special Regulations:** Reservoir only - Bag and possession limit for walleye is 4 fish, 18 inches or longer.

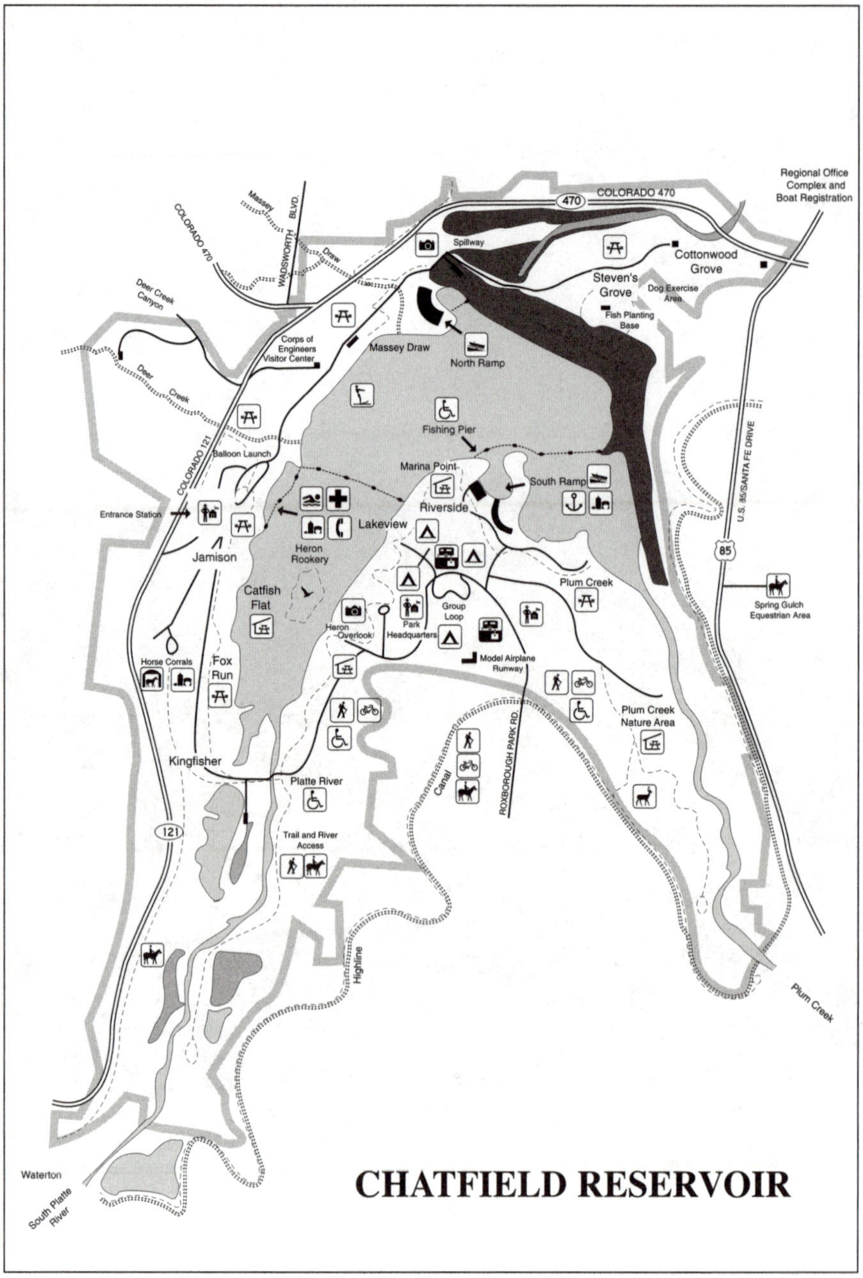

CHATFIELD RESERVOIR

## 59 Chatfield State Park, Ponds

**Location:** South of Chatfield Reservoir within park boundaries.
**Size:** 5 ponds; 140 acres total; 34 feet maximum depth.
**Fish:** Bluegill, bullhead, channel catfish, crappie, green sunfish, largemouth bass, sucker and yellow perch.
**Agency:** Colorado State Parks.
**Comments:** No boats except belly boats allowed for fishing. Parks Pass required. Free walk-in access possible from Hwy 75. No motorized access from parking areas. Artificial fish habitat structures in some ponds.

Chatfield Ponds

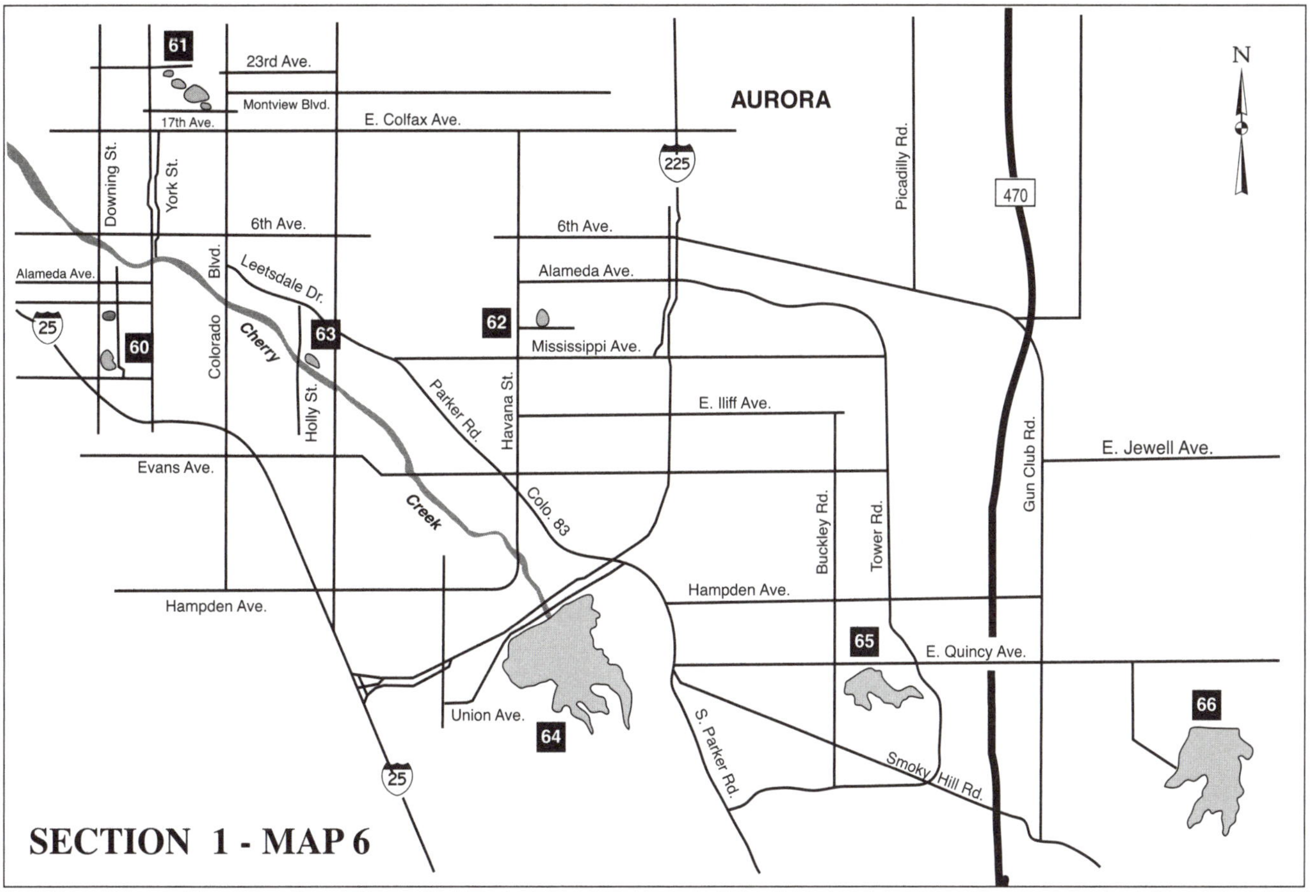

SECTION 1 - MAP 6

Chatfield Reservoir

## 60 Washington Park Lakes

**Location:** Northeast of the intersection of S. Downing Street and E. Louisiana Ave. The north lake (Smith Lake) has parking areas while the south lake (Grasmere Lake) has street parking only.
**Size:** Smith Lake - 19 acres; 12 feet maximum depth. Grasmere Lake - 19 acres; 10 feet maximum depth. Lily pad Lake - 1 acre; 8 feet maximum depth.
**Fish:** Smith Lake - Bluegill, bullhead, carp, channel catfish, crappie, gizzard shad, largemouth bass, pumpkinseed sunfish, rainbow trout (catchable size stocked in spring) and yellow perch.
**Grasmere Lake** - Bluegill, bullhead, carp, channel catfish, green sunfish, largemouth bass, and yellow perch.
**Agency:** Denver Parks & Recreation.
**Comments:** Open 5 a.m. to 11 p.m. No boats. Fishing piers at both lakes. Handicapped access to fishing pier on the south shore of Smith Lake. Recreation center, playground and restrooms. Hard surface foot trail.
**Special Regulation:** Lily Pad Pond is open to anglers 16 years of age or younger for fishing clinics.

## 61 City Park Lake

**Location:** North of 17th Ave. and west of Colorado Blvd. Parking area on the northwest side of the lake, between the park and the Denver Zoo.
**Size:** 25 acres; 8 feet maximum depth.
**Fish:** Bluegill, bullhead, carp, channel catfish, crappie, gizzard shad, green sunfish, largemouth bass, yellow perch and rainbow trout (catchable size stocked in spring).
**Agency:** Denver Parks & Recreation.
**Comments:** Open 5 a.m. to 11 p.m. No private boats. No fishing from rental boats. Restrooms. Hard surface foot trail.

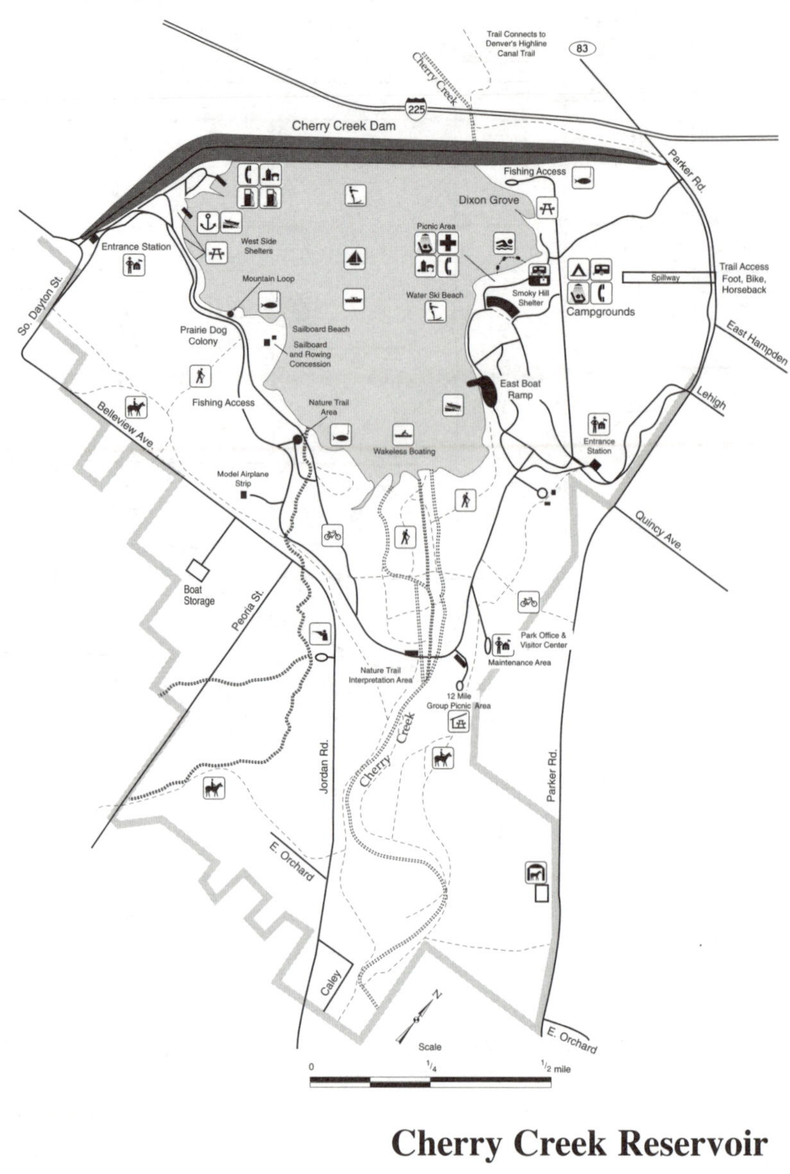

Fishing and picnic area at Cherry Creek State Park

Fishing and boating Cherry Creek Reservoir

## 62 Exposition Park Pond

**Location:** East Havana Street, north of E. Exposition Ave. at S. Moline Street. Foot trail in from Exposition.
**Size:** 5 acres; 5 feet maximum depth.
**Fish:** Bluegill, bullhead, carp and sucker.
**Agency:** Aurora Parks & Open Space.
**Comments:** Aurora Parks permit required. Open dawn to dusk. No boats. Good bullhead fishing. Extreme water level fluctuation.

## 63 Garland Park Lake (Lollipop Lake)

**Location:** Between S. Holly Street and S. Kerney Street north of Cherry Creek Drive North.
**Size:** 4 acres; 8 feet maximum.
**Fish:** Largemouth bass, orange spotted sunfish, sucker, yellow perch, bluegill, bullhead, channel catfish, crappie and green sunfish.
**Agency:** Denver Parks & Recreation.

## 64 Cherry Creek State Park

**Location:** I-225 to Parker Road. South on Parker to the east entrance. West entrance is off S. Yosemite Street. There are parking areas all around the reservoir.
**Size:** 800 acres; 30 feet maximum depth.
**Fish:** Northern pike, wiper, wiper, tiger muskie, walleye, channel catfish, rainbow trout (catchable size stocked),

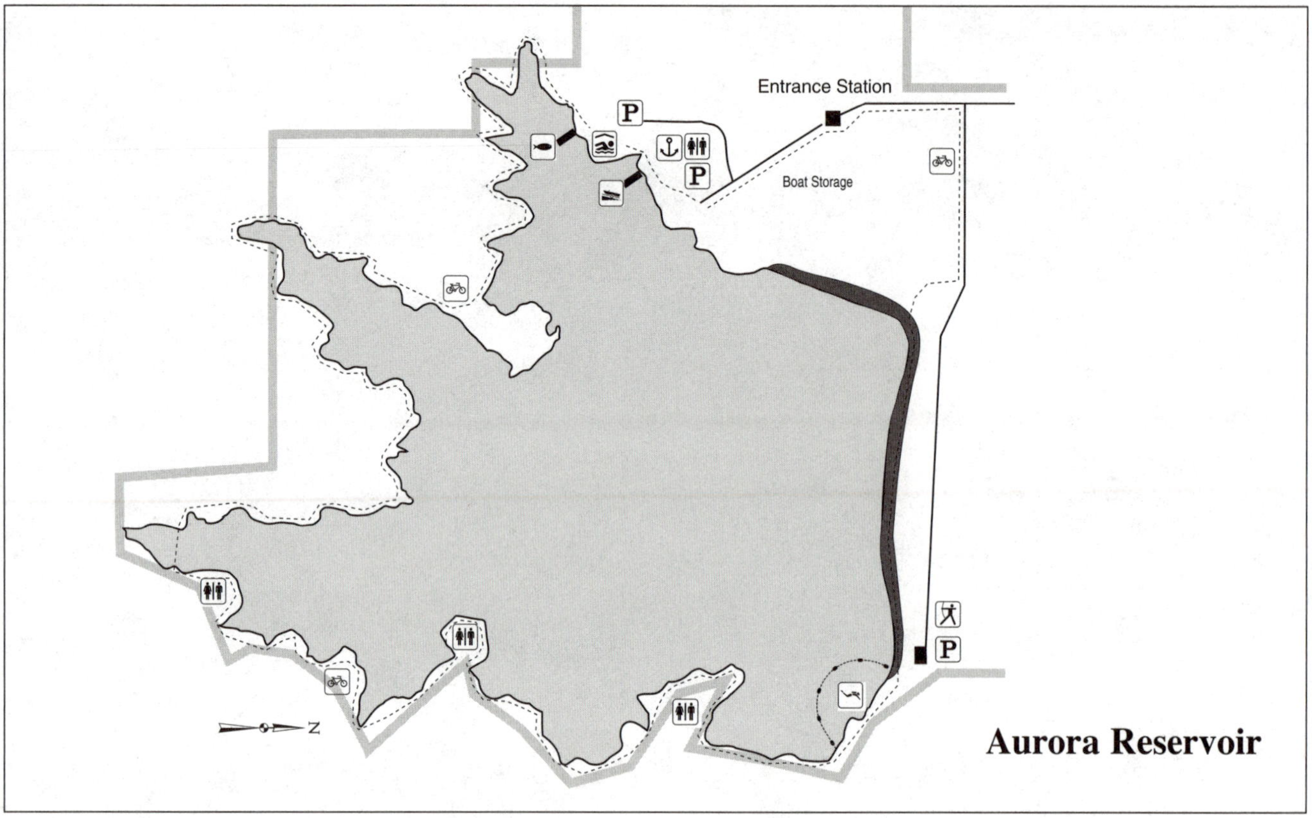

Entrance Station

Boat Storage

Aurora Reservoir

sucker, yellow perch, bluegill, bullhead, carp, crappie, gizzard shad, green sunfish and largemouth bass. Best time is April and May at night along the dams.
**Agency:** Colorado State Parks.
**Comments:** Open 24 hours. Boating, (Rentals available) camping. Fee area. Free walk-in fisherman access. Handicapped accessible fishing pier. State records for walleye. Ice fishing. Boat rentals. Marina. Boat ramps. May close due to capacity. Artificial fish habitat structures in lake. (See map page 38.) Camping.
**Special Regulations:** Bag and possession limit for walleye is 4 fish, 18 inches or longer.

## 65 Quincy Reservoir

**Location:** On E. Quincy Ave., 3 miles east of Parker Road. Parking area is south of Quincy on the northeast side of the reservoir.
**Size:** 160 acres; 58 feet maximum.
**Fish:** Brown trout, largemouth bass, rainbow trout (catchable-size stocked), sucker, tiger muskie and yellow perch.
**Agency:** City of Aurora Parks & Open Space.
**Comments:** Hours variable. Fee area. Aurora Park Permit required. Capacity is limited to 100 persons. Artificial fish habitat structures in the reservoir. Boat rental available. No boat ramp. No gas motored boats allowed. Waders allowed. Hours; 1/2 hour before sunrise to one hour after sunset. Restrooms, handicapped fishing dock.
**Special Regulations:** 1.Fishing by artificial flies or artificial lures only; 2. Bag, possession and size limit for trout is 2 fish; 3. All smallmouth and largemouth bass taken must be 15 inches in length or longer; 4. Ice fishing is prohibited; 5.Closed Nov. - Feb.; 6. Evening hours as posted; 7. Tiger muskie must be 40 inches or longer to keep.

## 66 Aurora Reservoir

**Location:** From Denver take I-225 to Parker Rd., go south to Quincy Ave., 8 miles east on Quincy to entrance of reservoir.
**Size:** 820 acres; 110 feet maximum depth.
**Fish:** Walleye, yellow perch, wiper, channel catfish, rainbow trout, brown trout, smelt, spot-tail shiner, crappie and largemouth bass.
**Agency:** Aurora Parks & Open Space.
**Comments:** Handicapped accessible fishing pier and restrooms, hard surface foot trail. Fee area. Ice fishing allowed (Shelters must be portable, have anglers name and address, and be removed nightly). Electric motors only, no gasoline motors allowed. Boat rental available. Open dawn to dusk. Artificial fish habitat structures in lake. Aurora entrance permit required. (See map above.)
**Special Regulation:** Two trout limit; All black bass must be 15 inches or longer. Bag and possession limit for walleye is 5 fish 15 inches or longer.

## Section 2

# Longmont/Boulder/ Broomfield Area

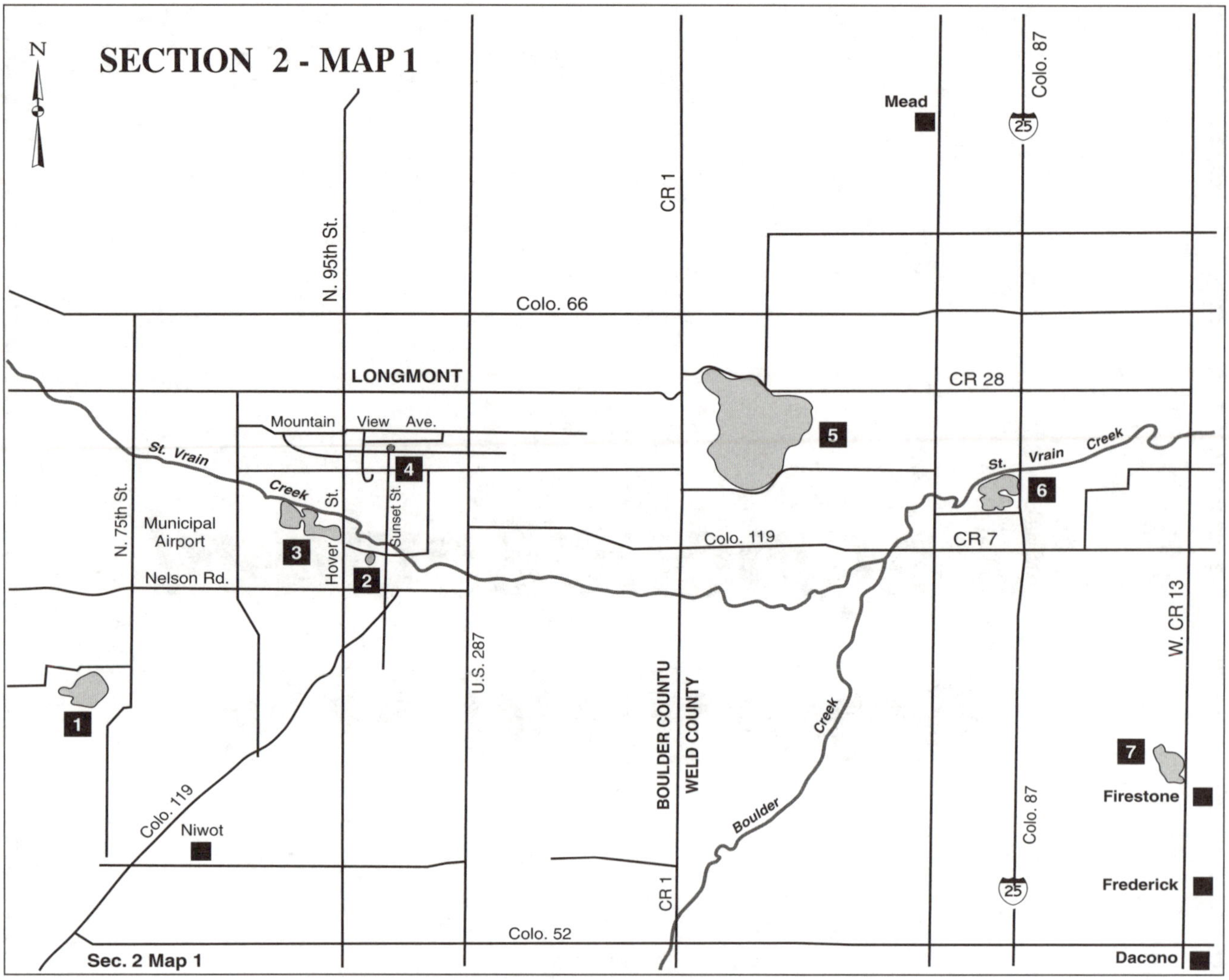

SECTION 2 - MAP 1

N

Mead
Colo. 87
25
CR 1
N. 95th St.
Colo. 66
LONGMONT
CR 28
Mountain View Ave.
St. Vrain Creek
5
4
N. 75th St.
Municipal Airport
Creek
Hover St.
Sunset St.
3
2
Nelson Rd.
Colo. 119
St. Vrain Creek
6
CR 7
W. CR 13
U.S. 287
1
BOULDER COUNTU
WELD COUNTY
Creek
Boulder
7
Firestone
Colo. 87
Colo. 119
Niwot
25
Frederick
CR 1
Colo. 52
Sec. 2 Map 1
Dacono

Fishing pier and picnic area at Lagerman Reservoir

## 1 Lagerman Reservoir

**Location:** Boulder County. 4 miles S.W. of Longmont between N 75th and N 63rd St.
**Size:** 116 acres.
**Fish:** Largemouth bass, walleye, crappie, bluegill, channel catfish, tiger muskie, bullhead, gizzard shad, fathead minnows and carp.
**Agency:** Boulder County Parks & Open Space.
**Comments:** Some boating allowed 7.5 h.p. or less wakeless speed. No swimming. Open dawn to dusk.

## 2 Fairgrounds Lake

**Location:** On Hover and Rogers Roads, in Longmont at Boulder County Fairgrounds.
**Size:** 16 acres.
**Fish:** Largemouth bass, bluegill and channel catfish.
**Agency:** Boulder County Parks & Open Space.
**Comments:** Offshore fishing and belly boats only. No boats. Catch & release only. Open dawn to dusk.

## 3 Golden Ponds

**Location:** West of Hover Rd. Located at 2651 Third Avenue.
**Fish:** Largemouth bass, trout and perch.
**Size:** 94 acres.
**Agency:** City of Longmont.
**Comments:** Outstanding wildlife: deer, beaver and birds. It includes 56 surface acres of water in four ponds. There are 9 picnic shelters, two restrooms facilities and 2.6 miles of trails. Open dawn to dusk.

## 4 Loomiller Pond

**Location:** Eleventh and Summer, in Longmont.
**Size:** 15 acres.
**Fish:** Trout, catfish and perch.

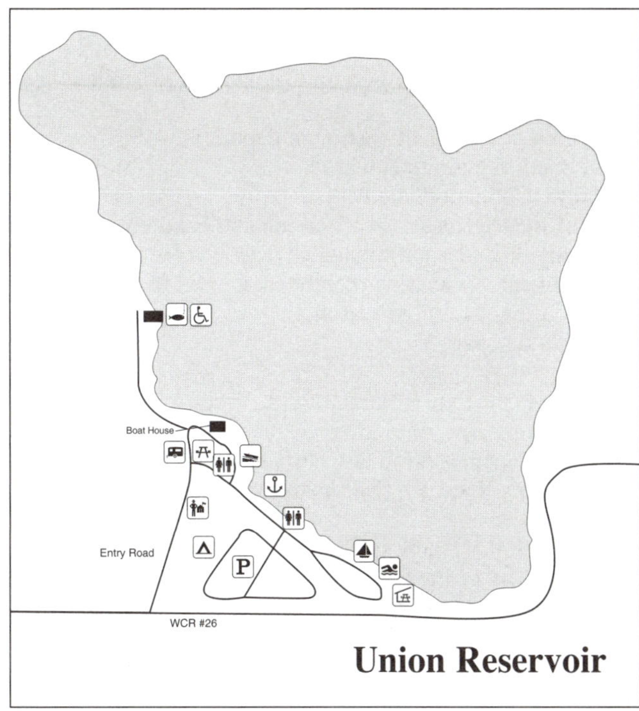


**Agency:** City of Longmont.
**Comments:** Colorado fishing licenses is required. Open dawn to dusk.

## 5 Union Reservoir

**Location:** West of I-25 on Colorado 119 to County Line Road 1, north 1 mile, east 1 mile to reservoir.
**Size:** 700 acres; 30 feet maximum depth.
**Fish:** Bluegill, crappie, and bass, wiper, trout and catfish.
**Agency:** City of Longmont. (See map above.)
**Comments:** Fishing pier, camping, restrooms.

**Union Reservoir**

# Section 2 - Map 1

## 6 St. Vrain State Park

**Location:** East of I-25 on Colorado 119, 1 mile north to park entrance.
**Size:** 130 acres; 6 feet maximum depth.
**Fish:** Catfish and rainbow trout.
**Agency:** Colorado State Parks.
**Special Restrictions:** Small sailing and hand-propelled craft only. Includes air inflated devices if more than one compartment. Swimming prohibited. Closed to vehicle traffic during waterfowl season.
(See map this page.)

## 7 Milavec Lake Recreation Area (Firestone Lake).

**Location:** 2 miles north of Colorado Highway 52 on Weld County Road 13 (Northwest on Fredrick.)
**Size:** 40 acres.
**Fish:** Trout (catchable size stocked), carp and crappie.
**Agency:** City of Fredrick.
**Comments:** Open one half hour before sunrise to one half hour after sunset. Fee area. No ice fishing. No open fires. No boats or flotation devices.

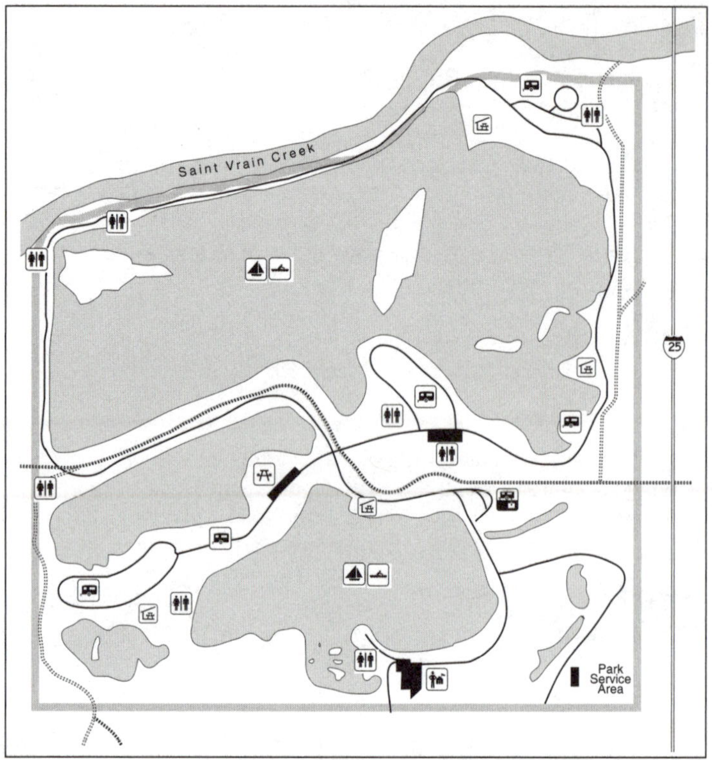


**St. Vrain State Park**

**St. Vrain State Park**

## SECTION 2 - MAP 2

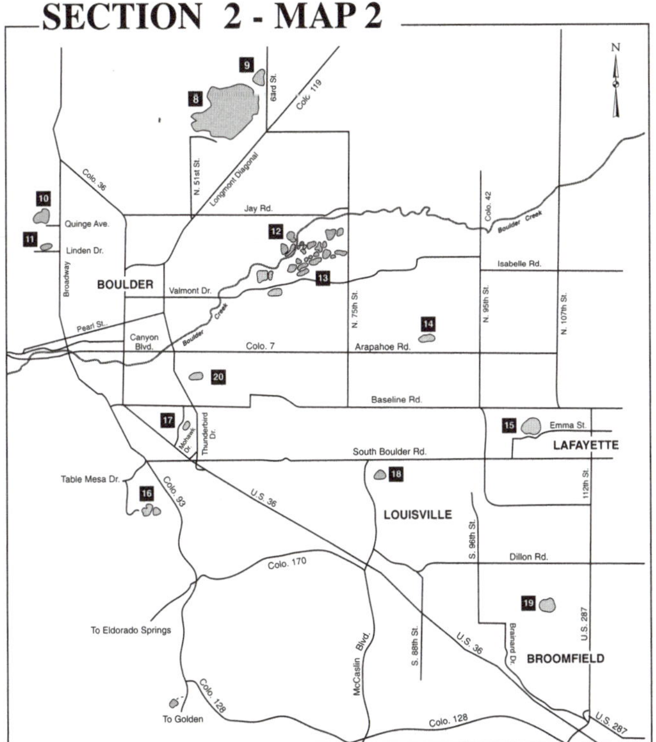

Piers on the beach at Boulder Reservoir

### 8 Boulder Reservoir

**Location:** From 28th Street (Hwy 36) go north to the Longmont Diagonal (Hwy 119) and turn northeast. At Jay Road turn west and then north almost immediately onto 51st Street. Access into the reservoir is east from 51st St.
**Size:** 540 acres; 40 feet maximum depth.
**Fish:** Walleye, channel catfish, black crappie, bluegill, largemouth bass, yellow perch, rainbow trout (catchable size stocked), carp and sucker.
**Agency:** Boulder Parks & Recreation Department.
**Comments:** Open 7 a.m. to dusk. Motorboats with city permit. Non-motorized boats need no permit. Excellent walleye fishery. Fee area but can park outside the area and walk-in free.

### 9 Coot Lake

**Location:** One-half mile northeast of Boulder Reservoir parking area. Two miles north of Longmont Diagonal (Hwy 119) on the west side of N. 63rd Street.
**Size:** 10 acres; 15 feet maximum depth.
**Fish:** Largemouth bass, crappie, bluegill, sucker, bullhead and smallmouth bass.
**Agency:** Boulder Parks & Recreation Department.
**Comments:** Open 7 a.m. to dusk. No boats.

Boulder Reservoir

## 10 Wonderland Lake

**Location:** N. Broadway to W. Poplar Ave. Turn west on Poplar to Wonderland Hill Road. Go north on Wonderland to the parking area.
**Size:** 34 acres; 13 feet maximum depth.
**Fish:** Largemouth bass, crappie, bullhead, yellow perch, carp and bluegill.
**Agency:** City of Boulder Parks & Open Space.
**Comments:** Open dawn to dusk. No boats. Walk-in fishing. Artificial fish habitat structures in lake. Dogs must be on hand-held leash. No glass allowed. Swimming and wading prohibited. Fishing only in designated areas.

Walden Ponds

## 11 Maxwell Lake

**Location:** From N. Broadway, one quarter mile west on Linden Ave. Walk in from Linden.
**Size:** 1.6 acres; 6 feet maximum depth.
**Fish:** bluegill, largemouth bass, bullhead, channel catfish and sucker.
**Agency:** Boulder Parks & Recreation Department.
**Comments:** Open 6 a.m. to 10 p.m. Non-motorized boats only.

## 12 Walden Ponds

**Location:** On 75th Street go one-half mile north of Valmont Road, cross the railroad tracks and turn west to the ponds. Immediately north of Sawhill Ponds.
**Size:** Picnic Pond (northeast) - 5.7 acres, 7 feet maximum depth.
Cottonwood Marsh (middle) - 30.3 acres; 8 feet maximum depth.
Duck Pond (south) - 6.3 acres; 5.6 feet maximum depth.
Island Lake and Bass Pond - 10 acres each; 12 feet maximum depth.
**Fish:** Largemouth bass, crappie, bluegill, carp, bullhead and channel catfish.
**Agency:** Boulder County Open Space.
**Comments:** Open dawn to dusk. Picnic Road restricted to handicapped and elderly by Boulder permit only. Permit available at the A-frame office at the park and at county annex located at 2045 13th Street.
**Special Regulations:** 1. All smallmouth and largemouth bass caught must be returned to the water immediately except in Picnic Pond. 2. Fishing by artificial flies and lures only on all waters except Picnic Pond. Wildlife viewing boardwalk on Cottonwood Marsh Pond.

## 13 Sawhill Ponds

**Location:** West of 75th Street between Valmont and Jay Roads. About 2 miles north of Arapaho Road.
**Size:** 16 ponds; from 1-10 acres; 16 feet maximum depth.
**Fish:** Largemouth bass, channel catfish, bluegill, crappie, yellow perch, bullhead and sucker.
**Agency:** Boulder Parks & Recreation Department.
**Comments:** Open dawn to dusk. No boats. Artificial habitat structures in some ponds.
**Special Regulation:** 1. All largemouth and smallmouth bass taken must be 15 inches in length or longer (All ponds). 2. Fishing by artificial lures only on all ponds except ponds #1 and #1a (eastern ponds).

## 14 Teller Lake

**Location:** Take Arapahoe Road (Hwy 7) west from Lafayette. Drive 1.4 miles west of 95th St. (Hwy 42). At sign for lake, turn north on dirt road for about .5 mile to parking lot. Lake is about .2 mile walk to the east.
**Size:** 28 acres; 20 feet maximum depth.
**Fish:** Yellow perch, largemouth bass, bluegill, crappie carp and bullhead.
**Agency:** City of Boulder Parks & Open Space.
**Special Regulations:** All largemouth and smallmouth bass taken must be 15 inches or longer.

## 15 Waneka Lake

**Location:** Lafayette. West of US 287, north of South Boulder Road. Access to the east entrance is via Hwy 287. At the intersection of Hwy 287 and Emma Street turn west on Emma. Parking area is on the corner of Emma and Caria Ave. The south entrance is via S. Boulder Road. Take S. Boulder Road to Ceres Drive. Turn north on Ceres to Caria Ave. At Caria go east to the parking area.
**Size:** 55 acres; 19 feet maximum depth.
**Fish:** Bluegill, carp, crappie largemouth bass, pumpkinseed sunfish and yellow perch.
**Agency:** Lafayette Parks & Recreation.
**Comments:** Open 7 a.m. to 10 p.m. Extreme water level fluctuation. Ice fishing. Artificial fish habitat in lake.
**Special Regulations:** 1. All smallmouth and largemouth bass taken must be 15 inches in length or longer.

Sawhill Ponds

## 16 Viele Reservoir

**Location:** South of the Table Mesa Shopping Center. From S. Broadway and Table Mesa Drive, go west on Table Mesa to Gillespie Street. Turn south on Gillespie to Harlow Platts Park. The lake is adjacent to the South Boulder Recreation Center.
**Size:** 6 acres; 15 feet maximum depth.
**Fish:** Yellow perch, bluegill, largemouth bass, crappie, carp, pumpkinseed sunfish, channel catfish and bullhead.
**Agency:** Boulder Parks & Recreation.
**Comments:** Open dawn to dusk. Non-motorized boats only. Hard surface foot trail.

## 17 Thunderbird Lake

**Location:** Mohawk and 47th Street.
**Size:** 2 acres; 10 feet maximum depth.
**Fish:** Largemouth bass, bluegill, crappie and sunfish.
**Agency:** Boulder Parks & Recreation.
**Comments:** Open dawn to dusk. No boats. Hard surface foot trail.

Picnic spot at Sawhill Ponds

Harper Lake

## 18 Harper Lake

**Location:** From Denver on U.S. 36 west to the Superior/Louisville exit. North on McCaslin Blvd. 1.5 miles to washington where parking is available.
**Size:** 31 acres; 39 feet maximum depth.
**Fish:** Rainbow trout (catchable size stocked), largemouth bass and green sunfish.
**Agency:** City of Louisville.
**Comments:** Non-motorized craft only.

## 19 Stearns Lake

**Location:** Northwest of Broomfield from Hwy 287 north to Dillon Rd. Dillon west to 104 th, south on 104th to Stearns Lake.
**Size:** 23.7 acres; 10 feet maximum depth.
**Fish:** Tiger muskie, channel catfish, largemouth bass, crappie and bluegill.
**Agency:** Boulder County Parks & Open Space.
**Comments:** No boats. No wading.
**Special Regulations:** Tiger muskies must be 30 inches in length. All smallmouth and largemouth bass taken must be 15 inches in length or longer.

## 20 Boulder Ponds

**Location:** Go east on S. Boulder Rd from intersection of Interstate 36 and S. Boulder Rd. Turn north on 55th St. to East Boulder Recreation Center. Ponds are south of recreation center.
**Size:** Two ponds: 1.0 acres each; 8 feet maximum depth.
**Fish:** Largemouth bass, bluegill, channel catfish and long nose sucker.
**Agency:** City of Boulder.
**Comments:** No boats.

Harper Lake fishing pier

## Section 3

# Mountain Lakes

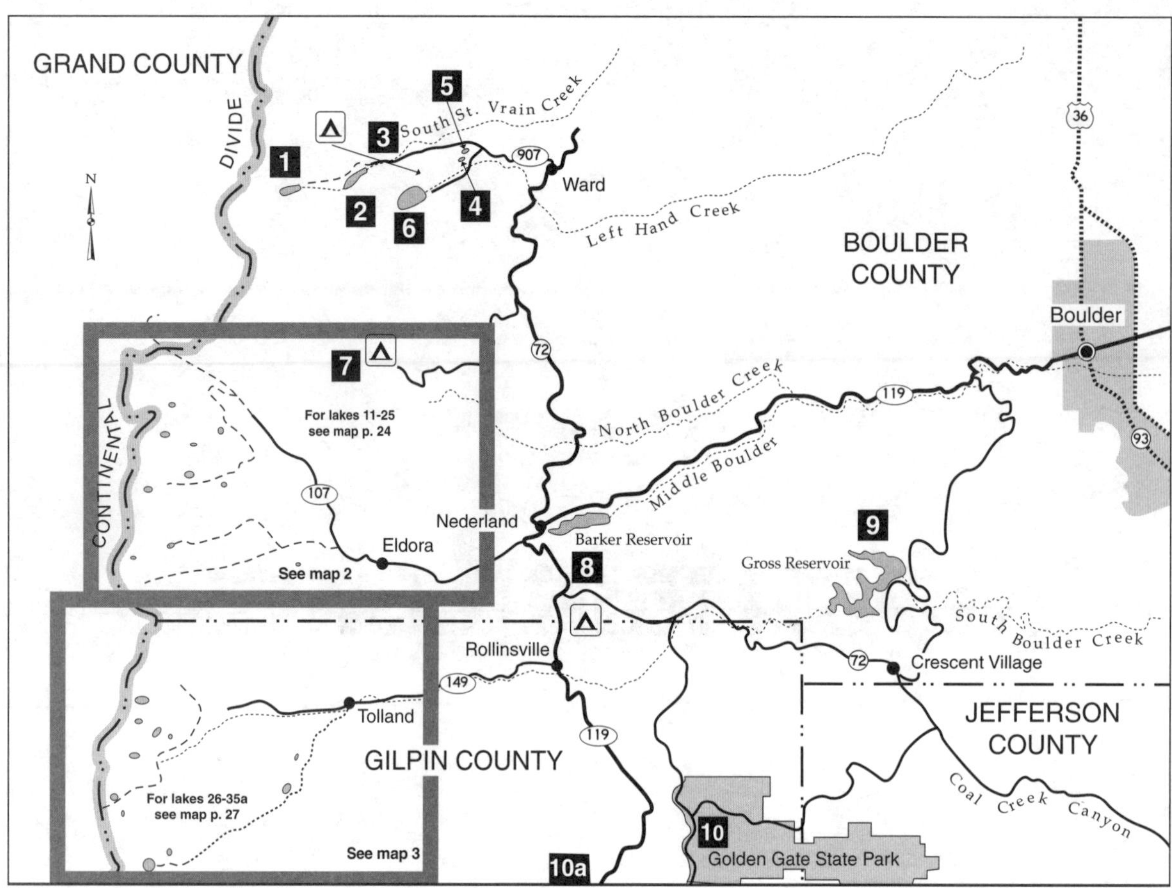


## SECTION 3 - MAP 1

### Mountain Lakes

The Mountain Lakes section is divided into five maps. Each lake is labeled by number on the maps and is accompanied by descriptions in the text. The descriptions of the mountain lakes include: general location, size and maximum depth, types of fish present, name of managing agency, and comments including USGS topo map, elevation, and any other information specific to the lake.

Mountain fishing spots near the metro area are often located on a mixture of national forest and private lands. Lakes, reservoirs, and stretches of stream may be public or private. Anglers are cautioned to respect private property and to avoid trespassing. Sometimes a private lake is surrounded by national forest land, but public fishing is not allowed.

## 1 Lake Isabelle

**Location:** Boulder County. Arapaho/Roosevelt National Forest. From Ward, go north one-quarter mile on Hwy 72 to Brainard Lake Road. Go west about 4 miles to Brainard Lake. Drive past Brainard Lake to trailhead. Hike west about one-quarter on Pawnee Pass Trail to Long Lake. Continue west on the trail (along north shore of Long Lake) about 2 miles to Lake Isabelle.
**Size:** 30 acres; 40 feet maximum depth.
**Fish:** Rainbow trout.
**Agency:** USFS-Boulder Ranger District.
**Comments:** USGS Ward quad; Elevation 10,868 feet. In Indian Peaks Wilderness Area. Non-motorized boats only. Fee area. Camping at Pawnee Campground near Brainard Lake by reservation.
**Special Regulations:** 1. Fishing by artificial flies or artificial lures only; 2. Bag, possession and size limit for trout is 2 fish.

## 2 Long Lake

**Location:** Boulder County. Arapaho/Roosevelt National Forest. From Ward, go north one-quarter mile on Hwy 72 to Brainard Lake Road. Go west about 4 miles to Brainard Lake. Drive past Brainard Lake to trailhead. Hike west about 1/4 mile on Pawnee Pass Trail to Long Lake.
**Size:** 39.5 acres; 22 feet maximum depth.
**Fish:** Rainbow trout and brook trout.
**Agency:** USFS-Boulder Ranger District.
**Comments:** USGS Ward quad; Elevation 10,500 feet. Non-motorized boats only. Fee area. Camping at Pawnee Campground near Brainard Lake by reservation.
**Special Regulations:** 1. Fishing by artificial flies or artificial lures only; 2. Bag and possession limit for trout is 2 fish; 3. Fishing is prohibited in the outlet stream of Long Lake to the bridge at the inlet at Brainard Lake from May 1 through July 15, as posted.

## 3 Brainard Lake

**Location:** Boulder County. Arapaho/Roosevelt National Forest. From Ward, go north one-quarter mile on Hwy 72 to Brainard Lake Road. Go west about 4 miles to Brainard Lake.
**Size:** 15.6 acres; 8 feet maximum depth.
**Fish:** Rainbow trout (catchable size stocked), brook and brown trout.
**Agency:** USFS-Boulder County Ranger District.
**Comments:** USGS Ward quad; Elevation 10,350 feet. Non-motorized boats only. Restrooms. Fee area. Camping at Pawnee Campground near Brainard Lake by reservation.

## 4 Moraine Lake

**Location:** Boulder County. Arapaho/Roosevelt National Forest. From Ward, go north on Hwy 72 one-quarter mile to Brainard Lake Road. Go west 2 miles past the turnoff for lefthand park. Moraine Lake is on the south beyond Red Rock Lake.
**Size:** 2.0 acres; 3.5 feet maximum depth.
**Fish:** Rainbow trout.
**Agency:** USFS-Boulder Ranger District.
**Comments:** USGS Ward quad; Elevation 10,150 feet. Non-motorized boats only.

## 5 Red Rock Lake

**Location:** Boulder County. Arapaho/Roosevelt National Forest. From Ward, go north on Hwy 72 one-quarter mile to Brainard Lake Road. Go west 2 miles past the turnoff for lefthand park. On the south side of the road is a parking area for Red Rock Lake.
**Size:** 6.5 acres; 3 feet maximum depth.
**Fish:** Rainbow trout (catchable size stocked).
**Agency:** USFS-Boulder Ranger District.
**Comments:** USGS Ward quad; Elevation 10,300 Grassy with lily pads. Non-motorized boats only.

Baker Reservoir in Nederland

## 6 Lefthand Creek Reservoir

**Location:** Boulder County. Arapaho/Roosevelt National Forest. From Ward, go north on Hwy 72 one-quarter mile to Brainard Lake Road. Go west 2 miles to Lefthand Park Road. Follow road southwest about 2 miles to the reservoir.
**Size:** 100 acres; 34 feet maximum depth.
**Fish:** Rainbow, brook, brown trout and splake.
**Agency:** USFS-Boulder Ranger District.
**Comments:** USGS Ward quad; Elevation 10,600 feet. Boats allowed, no gasoline motors.

## 7 Rainbow Lakes

**Location:** Boulder County. Arapaho/Roosevelt National Forest. From Ward, go south about 3.5 miles on Hwy 72. Turn west on gravel road. (First fork goes to the University of Colorado Camp.) Take south fork about 4 miles to Rainbow Lakes campground and trailhead.
**Size:** Ten beaver ponds; from 1 to 4 acres; 15 feet maximum depth.
**Fish:** Brook and rainbow trout.
**Agency:** USFS-Boulder Ranger District.
**Comments:** USGS-Ward quad; Elevation 10,200 feet. Forest Service campground. Trailhead for Arapaho Glacier Trail. Non-motorized boats only.

Springtime at Golden Gate Canyon State Park's Kriley Pond

Gross Reservoir

## 8 Barker Reservoir

**Location:** Boulder County. Arapaho/Roosevelt National Forest.
From Nederland, go one-half mile east along Hwy 119. The reservoir is on Middle Boulder Creek. From Boulder, go 15 miles west along Hwy 119.
**Size:** 380 acres; 100 feet maximum depth.
**Fish:** Rainbow trout (catchable size stocked), brook and brown trout, splake and sucker.
**Agency:** Public Service Company.
**Comments:** USGS Nederland quad; Elevation 8,200 feet. Fluctuation water storage reservoir. No boats or ice fishing.

## 9 Gross Reservoir

**Location:** Boulder County. Arapaho/Roosevelt National Forest.
From Boulder, drive west on Baseline Road to Flagstaff Mountain Road. Wind southwest for about 7 miles to Gross Reservoir. From Golden, drive 18 miles north on Hwy 93 to Boulder and turn west on Baseline Road. Follow directions from Boulder. Alternate route from Golden, drive 7 miles north on Hwy 93, then turn west on Hwy 72, Coal Creek Canyon. Drive about 10 miles northwest to Crescent Village. Drive north about 3 miles to Gross Reservoir. From Nederland, drive about 2.5 miles south on Hwy 119. Turn east on Hwy 72, and drive about 9 miles east to Crescent Village. Turn north and go about 3 miles to Gross Reservoir.
**Size:** 412 acres; 230 feet maximum depth.
**Fish:** Rainbow trout (catchable size stocked), brook, brown and lake trout, kokanee salmon and tiger muskie.
**Agency:** Denver Water Department.
**Comments:** USGS Tungsten and Eldorado Springs quads; Elevation 7,287 feet. Steep banked. No camping, no boating or floating devices. Fires in firepits on north side only.

Open 4 a.m. to 9 p.m. Ice fishing at own risk. Water level fluctuation.
**Special Regulations:** Kokanee snagging permitted September 1 through December 31. West side of reservoir is closed approx. Dec. 1 thru May 15, for critical wildlife habitat.

## 10 Golden Gate Canyon State Park Lakes

**Location:** Gilpin and Jefferson Counties. From Golden, drive north 1 mile on Hwy 93 to Golden Gate Canyon Road, then west 14 miles to the park. From Nederland, drive about 8 miles south on Hwy 119 to park entrance. Alternate route from Boulder, drive south on Hwy 93 to Golden Gate Canyon Road, and turn west 14 miles to the park. Also reached from Hwy 119 by turning east about 5 miles north of Black Hawk.
**Size:** 13 ponds; 15 acres total.
**Fish:** Rainbow trout (catchable size stocked), brown and brook trout.
**Agency:** Colorado State Parks.
**Comments:** USGS Blackhawk quad; Elevation 8,230 feet. No fishing in visitor center show pond. Park is a fee area. No boats. Ice fishing allowed on Kriley and Slough Ponds.

## 10a Central City Park Pond (Dorothy Lee)

**Location:** Gilpin County. From Highway 199 at Blackhawk go west on Eureka St. through Central City. Take a left onto Gilpin County Road 2. The pond is .5 miles on the left.
**Size:** 2 acres; 10 feet maximum depth.
**Fish:** Rainbow Tout (catchable-size stocked).
**Agency:** Central City.
**Comments:** USGS Central City quad; Elevation 8.940 feet. No boating allowed. Open during daylight hours.

## 10b Central City Park Pond (Chase Gulch Reservoir)

**Location:** Gilpin County. From Highway 199 at Blackhawk go west on Eureka St. through Central City. Continue to a right to Apex Road (Cty Rd. 3) and follow around to reservoir.
**Size:** 25 acres; 90 feet maximum depth.
**Fish:** Various trout species (including catchable-size rainbows).
**Agency:** Central City. (Call for opening date).
**Comments:** USGS Central City quad; Elevation 8,590 feet. Non-motorized boats only. Open during daylight hours.

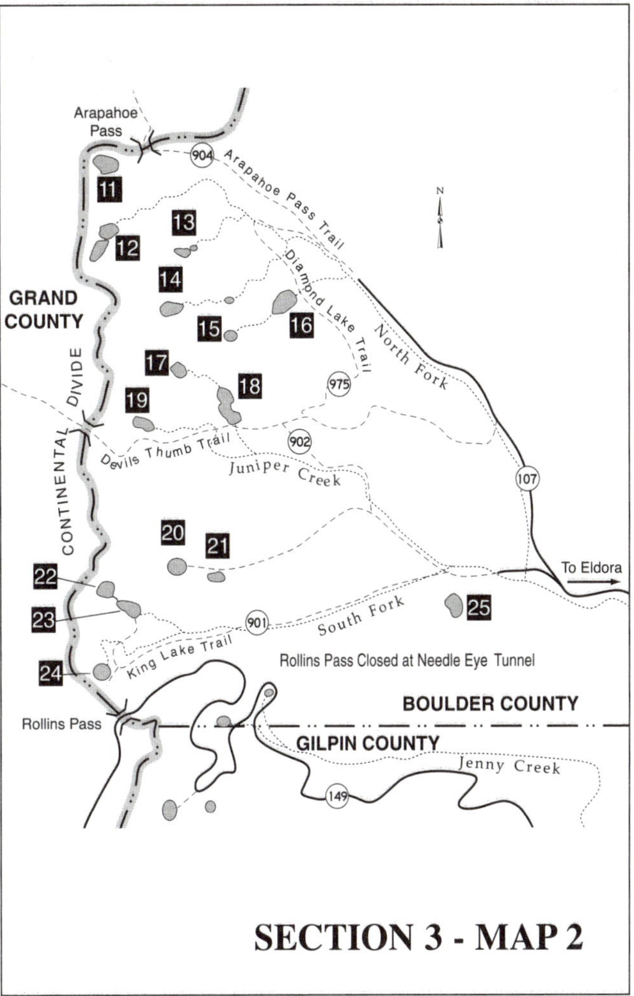


## 11 Lake Dorothy

**Location:** Boulder County. Arapaho/Roosevelt National Forest. From Nederland, go one-half mile south on Hwy 72-119. Turn west, go 4 miles to Eldora, continue 1 mile and take the north fork of the road, along the north fork of Middle Boulder Creek. Drive about 4 miles to the Fourth of July Campground. Hike north and northwest on Arapaho Pass Trail for about 3 miles. Lake Dorothy is in open country about one-half mile southwest of the summit.
**Size:** 16 acres; 100 feet maximum depth.
**Fish:** Cutthroat trout.
**Agency:** USFS-Boulder Ranger District.
**Comments:** USGS Monarch Lake quad; Elevation 12,100 feet. Indian Peaks Wilderness Area. Non-motorized boats.

## 12 Neva Lakes

**Location:** Boulder County. Arapaho/Roosevelt National Forest. From Nederland, go one-half mile south on Hwy 72-119. Turn west, go 4 miles to Eldora, continue 1 mile and take the north fork of the road, along the north fork of Middle Boulder Creek. Hike north on Arapaho Pass Trail. After one-half mile take the west fork, Diamond Lake Trail. Go northwest about one-half mile where the trail crosses a small stream and then curves southeast. Cut off at the second stream, north fork of Middle Boulder Creek, and follow it cross county for 2 miles. No trail, use of a topo map advised.

**Size:** Upper Lake - 8.6 acres; 61 feet maximum depth. Lower Lake - 10.0 acres; 49 feet maximum depth.
**Fish:** Cutthroat trout.
**Agency:** USFS-Boulder Ranger District.
**Comments:** USGS Monarch Lake quad; Elevation 11,800 feet. Non-motorized boats only. No fish in upper lake.

## 13 Diamond Lake - Upper

**Location:** Boulder County. Arapaho/Roosevelt National Forest. From Nederland, go one-half mile south on Hwy 72-119. Turn west, go 4 miles to Eldora, continue 1 mile and take the north fork of the road, along the north of Middle Boulder Creek. Dive about 4 miles to the Fourth of July Trailhead. Hike north on Arapaho Pass Trail. After one-half mile take the west fork, Diamond Lake Trail. Follow trail 904 & 975 to Diamond Lake. Follow obscure trail upstream to Upper Diamond.
**Size:** 6 acres; 17 feet maximum depth.
**Fish:** Cutthroat trout.
**Agency:** USFS - Boulder Ranger District.
**Comments:** USGS East Portal quad; Elevation 11,720 feet. Non-motorized boats only.
**Helpful Hints:** Try fishing the outlet in areas as soon as the ice goes out in late June or early July for nice sized cutthroat attempting to spawn. Gold or Silver Panther Martin Spinners work extremely well at this time and throughout the summer. Fly fishing with two flies (A dry and wet dropper) off the shoal edges can be productive. Dark colored flies size 16 or smaller seem to work best.

## 14 Deep Lake

**Location:** Boulder County. Arapaho/Roosevelt National Forest. From Nederland, go one-half mile south on Hwy 72-119. Turn west, go 4 miles to Eldora, continue 1 mile and take the north fork of the road, along the north fork of Middle Boulder Creek. Drive about 4 miles to the Fourth of July Trailhead. Hike north on Arapaho Pass Trail about 1/4 mile and take the west fork, Diamond Lake Trail. Go northwest about one-half mile. Trail crosses a small stream and then curves southwest. Cut off at the second stream, north fork at Middle Boulder Creek, and follow it cross country about 1/8 mile. Head west at tributary, follow for 3/4 mile.
**Size:** 4.9 acres; 20 feet maximum depth.
**Fish:** Cutthroat and rainbow trout.
**Agency:** USFS - Boulder Ranger District.
**Comments:** USGS East Portal and Monarch Lake quads. Altitude 11,320 feet. Rough country. Non-motorized boats.

## 15 Banana Lake

**Location:** Boulder County. Arapaho/Roosevelt National Forest. From Nederland, go one-half mile south on Hwy 72-119. Turn west, go 4 miles to Eldora, continue one mile and take the north fork of the road, along the north fork Middle Boulder Creek. Drive about 4 miles to the Fourth of July Trailhead. Follow trail 904 and 975 to Diamond Lake, follow obscure trail upstream for one-half mile. Use topo map advised.
**Size:** 1.5 acres; 13 feet maximum depth.
**Fish:** Cutthroat trout.
**Agency:** USFS-Boulder Ranger District.
**Comments:** USGS East Portal quad; Elevation 11,320 feet. No boats.

## 16 Diamond Lake

**Location:** Boulder County. Arapaho/Roosevelt National Forest. From Nederland, go one-half mile south on Hwy 72-119. Turn west, go 4 miles to Eldora, continue 1 mile and take the north fork of the road, along the north fork Middle Boulder Creek. Drive about 4 miles to the Fourth of July Trailhead. Follow trail 904 and 975 to lake.
**Size:** 14 acres; 17 feet maximum depth.
**Fish:** Brook, cutthroat, lake and rainbow trout.
**Agency:** USFS-Boulder Ranger District.
**Comments:** USGS East Portal quad; Elevation 10, 920 feet. In Indian Peaks Wilderness area. Non-motorized boats.

## 17 Storm Lake

**Location:** Boulder County. Arapaho/Roosevelt National Forest. From Nederland, go one-half mile south on Hwy 72-119. Turn west, and go 4 miles to Eldora, continue 1 mile to the Hessie trailhead. Walk west about 5 miles on trail 902 to Jasper Lake. From north end of Jasper, follow inlet stream one-half mile northwest to Storm Lake.
**Size:** 7 acres; 22 feet maximum depth.
**Fish:** Cutthroat trout.
**Agency:** USFS-Boulder Ranger District.
**Comments:** USGS East Portal quad; Elevation 11,440 feet. Non-motorized boats only.

## 18 Jasper Lake

**Location:** Boulder County. Arapaho/Roosevelt National Forest. From Nederland, go one-half mile south on Hwy 72-119. Turn west, and go 4 miles to Eldora, continue one mile to Forest Route 109 to Hessie Trailhead. Walk west about 1.5 miles then take the north fork. Go up the trail one mile, past mine diggings, and take the north fork again. Continue north and west for 2.5 miles to Jasper Lake.
**Size:** 21 acres; 36 feet maximum depth.
**Fish:** Brook, brown and cutthroat trout.
**Agency:** USFS-Boulder Ranger District.
**Comments:** USGS Nederland and East Portal quads; Elevation 10,814 feet. In Indian Peaks Wilderness area. Non-motorized boats only.

## 19 Devil's Thumb Lake

**Location:** Boulder County. Arapaho/Roosevelt National Forest. From Nederland, go one-half mile south on Hwy 72-119. Turn west, go 4 miles to Eldora, continue one mile on Forest Route 109 to Hessie Trailhead. Walk west about 1.5 miles and then take the north fork. Go up the trail one mile, past mine diggings, and take north fork again. Continue north and west for 2.5 miles to Jasper Lake. Follow the trail 902 west for 1 mile to the lake.
**Size:** 11.5 acres; 37 feet maximum depth.
**Fish:** Cutthroat trout.
**Agency:** USFS-Boulder Ranger District.
**Comments:** USGS East Portal quads; Elevation 11,260 feet. In Indian Peaks Wilderness Area. Non-motorized boats.

## 20 Skyscraper Reservoir

**Location:** Boulder County. Arapaho/Roosevelt National Forest. From Nederland, go one-half mile south on Hwy 72-119. Turn west, go 4 miles to Eldora. Continue

1 mile on Forest Route 109 to the Hessie Trailhead. Hike west about 1.5 miles then take the north fork. Go up the trail 1 mile, past mine diggings, to the next fork. Go west 2 miles to Woodland Lake. Go a few hundred yards more to Skyscraper Reservoir.
**Size:** 12.9 acres; 28 feet maximum depth.
**Fish:** Cutthroat trout.
**Agency:** USFS-Boulder Ranger District.
**Comments:** USGS East Portal quads; Elevation 11,221 feet. In Indian Peaks Wilderness Area. Non-motorized boats only.

## 21 Woodland Lake

**Location:** Boulder County. Arapaho/Roosevelt National Forest. From Nederland, go one-half mile south on Hwy 72-119. Turn west, and go 4 miles to Eldora. Continue 1 mile on Forest Route 109 to the Hessie Trailhead. Hike west about 1.5 miles then take the north fork. Go up the trail 1 mile, past mine diggings, to the next fork. Go west 2 miles to Woodland Lake.
**Size:** 10 acres; 7 feet maximum depth.
**Fish:** Cutthroat trout and grayling.
**Agency:** USFS - Boulder Ranger District.
**Comments:** USGS East Portal quads; Elevation 10,972 feet. In Indian Peaks Wilderness Area. Non-motorized boats only.

## 22 Bob Lake

**Location:** Boulder County. Arapaho/Roosevelt National Forest. From Nederland, go one-half mile south on Hwy 72-119. Turn west, and go 4 miles to Eldora. Continue 1 mile on Forest Route 109 to the Hessie Trailhead. Walk 5 miles west on trail 901, then southwest at the fork, following the south fork of Middle Boulder Creek. At intersection with north-south trail go north one-half mile plus, to Betty Lake. From trail along west shore of Betty Lake continue one-eighth mile to Bob Lake. Can also be reached by hiking north from Rollins Pass.
**Size:** 8.5 acres; 71 feet maximum depth.
**Fish:** Cutthroat trout.
**Agency:** USFS - Boulder Ranger District.
**Comments:** USGS East Portal quad; Elevation 11,600 feet. In Indian Peaks Wilderness Area. Non-motorized boats only.

## 23 Betty Lake

**Location:** Boulder County. Arapaho/Roosevelt National Forest. From Nederland, go one-half mile south on Hwy 72-119. Turn west, and go 4 miles to Eldora. Continue one mile on Forest Route 109 to Hessie Trailhead. Walk 5 miles west, then southwest at the fork, following the south fork of Middle Boulder Creek. At intersection with north-south trail go north one-half mile plus, to Betty Lake. Can also be reached by hiking north from Rollins Pass. Use East Portal quad.
**Size:** 8.5 acres; 11 feet maximum depth.
**Fish:** Cutthroat trout.
**Agency:** USFS-Boulder Ranger District.
**Comments:** USGS Nederland and East Portal quads; Elevation 11,500 feet. In Indian Peaks Wilderness Area. Non-motorized boats only.

## 24 King Lake

**Location:** Boulder County. Arapaho/Roosevelt National Forest. From Nederland, go one-half mile south on Hwy 72-119. Turn west and go 4 miles to Eldora. Continue 1 mile on Forest Route 109 to Hessie trailhead. Walk 6 miles west, then southwest at the fork, following the south fork of Middle Boulder Creek. At intersection with north-south trail go south about one-quarter mile to King Lake. Can also be reached by hiking north one-half mile from Rollins Pass summit. Use East Portal quad.
**Size:** 11.5 acres; 61 feet maximum depth.
**Fish:** Cutthroat and rainbow trout.
**Agency:** USFS-Boulder Ranger District.
**Comments:** USGS Nederland and East Portal quads; Elevation 11,431 feet. In Indian Peaks Wilderness Area. Non-motorized boats only.

## 25 Lost Lake

**Location:** Boulder County. Arapaho/Roosevelt National Forest. From Nederland, go one-half mile south on Hwy 72-119. Turn west, and go 4 miles to Eldora. Continue 1 mile on Forest Route 109 to Hessie Trailhead. Hike west on the trail 902 and then southwest at the fork, total distance under 2 miles.
**Size:** 8.6 acres; 14 feet maximum depth.
**Fish:** Rainbow and brook trout.
**Agency:** USFS-Boulder Ranger District.
**Comments:** USGS Nederland quad; Elevation 9,740 feet. Non-motorized boats only.

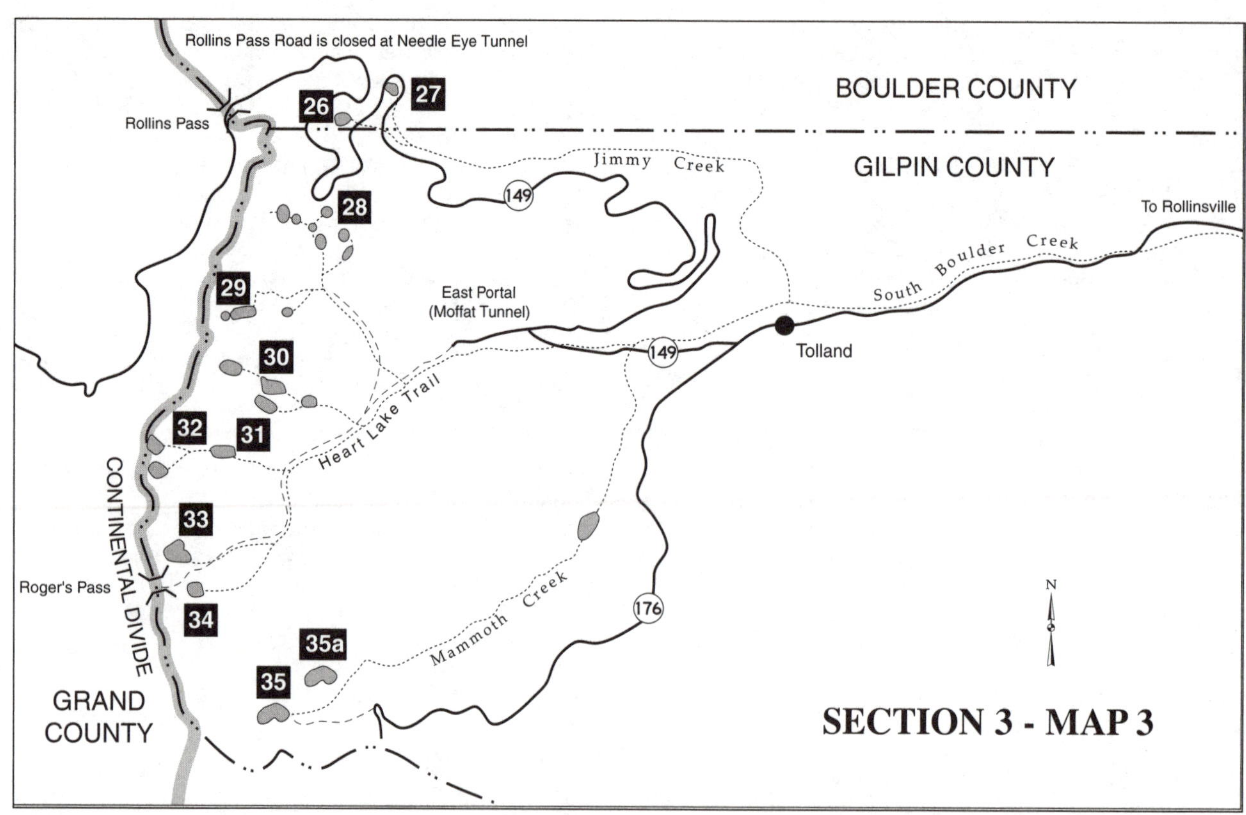

Jenny Lake

## 26 Jenny Lake

**Location:** Boulder County. Arapaho/Roosevelt National Forest. From Rollinsville, drive west about 7 miles on Forest Route 149. Turn north on old railroad grade. (Before East Portal.) Drive about ten miles up Rollins Pass Road (Forest Route 149) to Yankee Doodle Lake. Drive 1 mile further to Jenny Lake.
**Size:** 4.5 acres; 9 feet maximum depth.
**Fish:** Brook and rainbow trout (catchable size stocked.) and sucker.
**Agency:** USFS-Boulder Ranger District.
**Comments:** USGS East Portal quads; Elevation 10,917 feet. Forest Road 149 (Rollins Pass Rd.) is closed at Needle Eye Tunnel. Non-motorized boats only. Check road conditions.

## 27 Yankee Doodle Lake

**Location:** Boulder County. Arapaho/Roosevelt National Forest. From Rollinsville, drive west about 7 miles on Forest Route 149. Turn north on old railroad grade. (Before East Portal.) Drive about 10 miles up Rollins Pass Road (Forest Route 149) to Yankee Doodle Lake.
**Size:** 5.7 acres; 24 feet maximum depth.
**Fish:** Rainbow (catchable size stocked) and brook trout.
**Agency:** USFS-Boulder Ranger District.
**Comments:** USGS East Portal quad; Elevation 10,711 feet. Inquire locally about current road conditions. Boats allowed. Forest Road 149 (Rollins Pass Rd.) is closed at Needle Eye Tunnel. Artificial fish habitat structures.

## 28 Forest Lakes

**Location:** Boulder County. Arapaho/Roosevelt

Yankee Doodle Lake from above

**High-elevation Yankee Doodle Lake**

National Forest. From Rollinsville, drive west about 8 miles on Forest Route 149 to East Portal. Park by tunnel. On the south side of the road walk through the gate. (Gate may be locked). Hike 1 mile southwest on the road, to the intersection with South Boulder Creek Pack Trail. Turn north and go up the trail 1.5 miles. (At 0.5 mile the trail crosses a creek). Where the creeks meet, take the north fork. Hike .5 mile north cross country to the first lake, or another .5 mi. to the second. Can also be reached by hiking south .5 mile from Rollins Pass Road. (FDR 149) south of Jenny Lake.
**Size:** Upper - 4.3 acres; 8.2 feet maximum depth.
Lower - 2.7 acres; 3.2 feet maximum depth.
**Fish:** Brook trout.
**Agency:** USFS - Boulder Ranger District.
**Comments:** USGS East Portal quad; Elevation 10,800 feet. Small forest ponds. Non-motorized boats only.

## 29 Arapaho Lakes

**Location:** Gilpin County. Arapaho/Roosevelt National Forest. From Rollinsville, drive about 8 miles on Forest Route 149 to East Portal. Park by tunnel. On the south side of the road walk through the gate (Gate may be locked). Hike one mile southwest on the road, to intersection with South Boulder Creek Trail. Turn north and go up the trail 1.5 miles. (At 0.5 miles the trail crosses a creek.) Where the creeks meet take the west fork. Follow the stream three-quarters of a mile west to the first lake. There are 2 more lakes to the west directly up stream. (After taking the west fork, at about 1/8 a mile a small tributary comes in from the south, there is a small pond about one-half mile up stream.)
**Size:** East - 9.8 acres; 49.2 feet maximum depth.
Middle - 4 acres; 15 feet maximum depth.
West - 2.5 acres; 16.4 feet maximum depth.
**Fish:** Cutthroat and golden trout.
**Agency:** USFS-Boulder Ranger District.
**Comments:** USGS East Portal quad; Elevation 11,580 feet. Non-motorized boats only.

## 30 Crater Lakes

**Location:** Gilpin County. Arapaho/Roosevelt National

Forest. From Rollinsville, drive west about 8 miles on Forest Route 149 to East Portal. Park by tunnel. On the south side of the road walk through the gate (Gate may be locked). Hike 1 mile southwest on road, to intersection with South Boulder Creek Trail. Turn south into the clearing. Hike west, upstream for 1/2 mile to the first lake. No trail, use of topo map advised.
**Size:** East - 5.7 acres; 4 feet maximum depth.
Southeast - 8.6 acres; 29 feet maximum depth.
Middle - 14.0 acres; 14 feet maximum depth.
West - 8.5 acres; 58 feet maximum depth.
**Fish:** Rainbow, brook, brown and cutthroat trout.
**Agency:** USFS - Boulder Ranger District.
**Comments:** USGS East Portal quad; Elevation 11,000 feet. Non-motorized boats only.
**Helpful Hints:** The most productive way to fish these four lakes is from a float tube. A tremendous fly ant hatch (size 14-16) occurs in August on the lower three lakes. The best time to fish the upper lake for cutthroat is after the ice melts in late June or early July. At this time cutthroat often cruise the shallow, shoals looking for food and spawning habitat.

## 31 Clayton Lake

**Location:** Gilpin County. Arapaho/Roosevelt National Forest. From Rollinsville, drive west about 8 miles on Forest Route 149 to East Portal. Park by tunnel. On the south side of the road walk through gate (Gate may be locked). Hike 1 mile southwest on road, to intersection with South Boulder Creek Trail. Turn south, cross creek, and hike about 1 mile to another creek. Turn west and follow the creek (no trail) for 1/2 mile to Clayton Lake. Use topo map advised. (See Crater Lake)
**Size:** 5 acres; 4 feet maximum depth.
**Fish:** Cutthroat trout.
**Agency:** USFS-Boulder Ranger District.
**Comments:** USGS East Portal quad; Elevation 11,560 feet. Non-motorized boats only.

## 32 Iceberg Lakes

**Location:** Gilpin County. Arapaho/Roosevelt National Forest. From Rollinsville, drive west about 8 miles on Forest Route 149 to East Portal. Park by tunnel. On the south side of the road walk through the gate (Gate may be locked). Hike 1 mile southwest on road, to intersection with South Boulder Creek Trail. Turn south, cross creek, and hike about one mile to another creek. Turn west and follow the creek (no trail) for 1/2 mile to Clayton Lake. Continue one-half mile west along the creek, then take either fork another 1/2 mile to the lakes.
**Size:** North Lake - 10 acres; 77 feet maximum depth.
South Lake - 6 acres; 100 feet maximum depth.
**Fish:** Cutthroat trout.
**Agency:** USFS-Boulder Ranger District.
**Comments:** USGS East Portal quad; Elevation 11,500 feet. Non-motorized boats only. No fish in south lake.

## 33 Heart Lake

**Location:** Gilpin County. Arapaho/Roosevelt National Forest. From Rollinsville, drive west about 8 miles on Forest Route 149 to East Portal. Park by tunnel. On the south side of the road walk through gate (Gate may be locked). Hike 1 mile southwest on road, to intersection with South Boulder Creek Trail. Turn south, cross creek, and hike about 1 mile. Cross another creek and continue south three quarters of a mile, follow the trail west for one-half mile. Trail crosses stream turn off and hike west following stream for one-quarter mile to Heart Lake.
**Size:** 17 acres; 52 feet maximum depth.
**Fish:** Cutthroat trout.
**Agency:** USFS-Boulder Ranger District.
**Comments:** USGS East Portal quad; Elevation 12,218 feet. Trail continues west over Roger Pass. Non-motorized boats only.

## 34 Rogers Pass Lake

**Location:** Gilpin County. Arapaho/Roosevelt National Forest. From Rollinsville, drive west about 8 miles on Forest Route 149 to East Portal. Park by tunnel. On the south side of the road walk through gate (Gate may be locked). Hike one mile southwest on road, to intersection with South Boulder Creek Trail. Turn south, cross creek, and hike about 1 mile. Cross another creek and continue south three-quarters of a mile, follow the trail west for one-half a mile. Trail crosses stream. Stay on trail a short distance until Rogers Pass Lake is seen just to the south of the trail. It is before Rogers Pass.
**Size:** 5.6 acres; 6.5 feet maximum depth.
**Fish:** Cutthroat trout.
**Agency:** USFS-Boulder Ranger District.
**Comments:** USGS Empire quad; Elevation 11,200 feet. Non-motorized boats only.

## 35 James Peak Lake

**Location:** Gilpin County. Arapaho/Roosevelt National Forest. From Rollinsville, drive west 5.5 miles on Forest Route 149 to Tolland. Turn left on Forest Route 176. Go about 1.5 miles to triple fork. (Left fork goes to Elk park). Take right fork toward Kingston Peak and James Peak, about 4 miles to James Peak trailhead. Hike down the trail, about 1 mile west to James Peak Lake.
**Size:** 10 acres; 10 feet maximum depth.
**Fish:** Cutthroat trout.
**Agency:** USFS-Boulder Ranger District.
**Comments:** USGS Empire and East Portal quads; Elevation 11,100 feet. Non-motorized boats only.

## 35a Little Echo Lake

**Location:** Gilpin County, Arapaho/Roosevelt Nat. Forest. From Rollinsville west 5 mi. on Forest Rd 149 to Tolland. South on Forest Rd. 176 about 1.5 mi. to triple fork. (Left fork goes to Elk Park.) Take west fork towards Kingston Peak and James Peak about 4 mi. to James Peak Trailhead. Take trail #804 about 1.5 mi. west to Echo Lake.
**Size:** 13 acres; 96 feet maximum depth.
**Fish:** Rainbow and lake trout.
**Agency:** Central City.
**Comments:** USGS Empire and East Portal Quads; Elevation 11,100 feet. Non-motorized boats only.
**Helpful Hints:** This lake has naturally sustained lake trout population. Although most of the fish are smaller (Up to 14 inches), a unique angling opportunity exists to catch them on dry flies. Matching a spectacular flying ant hatch (size 14-16) in August while fishing from a float tube can be effective. (Fish often feed in the middle of the lake.)

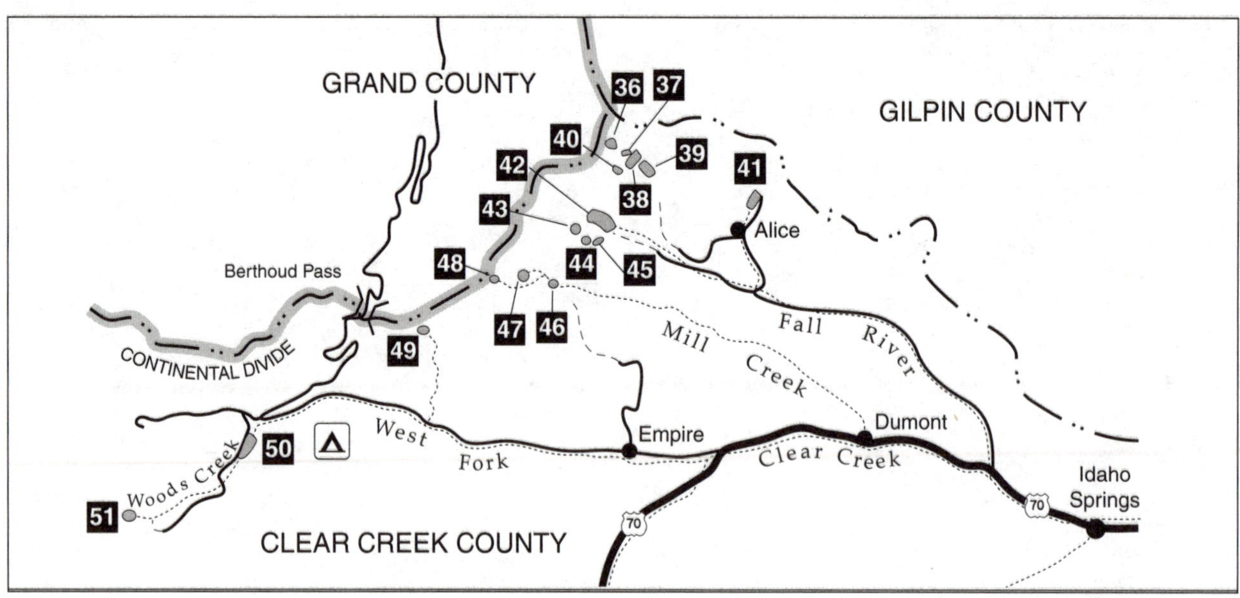


SECTION 3 - MAP 4

## 36 Ice Lake

**Location:** Clear Creek County. Arapaho/Roosevelt National Forest.
West on I-70 about 2 miles past Idaho Springs take exit 238, Fall River Road. Drive north on Fall River Road for 9 miles to the town of Alice. Turn left on Silver Creek then right on Texas Drive past the "Glory Hole Mine". Take first dirt road right after the mine (rough road). Passing by Steuart Lake hike .2 mile to Ohman Lake. Ice Lake is .2 miles past Ohman Lake.
**Size:** 12 acres; 102 feet maximum depth.
**Fish:** Cutthroat trout.
**Agency:** USFS-Clear Creek Ranger District.
**Comments:** USGS Empire quad; Elevation 12,200 feet. Ice stays on very late. Non-motorized boats only.

## 37 Steuart Lake

**Location:** Clear Creek County. Arapaho/Roosevelt National Forest. West on I-70 about 2 miles past Idaho Springs take exit 238, Fall River Road. Drive north on Fall River Road for 9 miles to the town of Alice. Turn left on Silver Creek then right on Texas Drive past the "Glory Hole Mine" sign. Take first dirt road after the mine (rough road). Hike around west side of Loch Lomond and uphill next to inlet stream about 1 mile to Reynolds Lake. Turn north and hike around the east side of Reynolds Lake then .1 mile to Steuart Lake.
**Size:** 7 acres; 15 feet maximum depth.
**Fish:** Brook and lake trout.
**Agency:** Agriculture Ditch and Reservoir Company.
**Comments:** USGS Empire quad; Elevation 11,400 feet. No boats.

## 38 Reynolds Lake

**Location:** Clear Creek County. Arapaho/Roosevelt National Forest. West on I-70 about 2 miles past Idaho Springs take exit 238, Fall River Road. Drive north on Fall River Road for 9 miles to the town of Alice. Turn left on Silver Creek then right on Texas Drive past the "Glory Hole Mine". Take first dirt road right after the mine (rough road). Hike around west side of Loch Lomond Lake and

**Loch Lomond Lake located above timberline**

uphill to next inlet stream about .1 mile to Reynolds Lake.
**Size:** 3 acres; 28 feet maximum depth.
**Fish:** Brook trout.
**Agency:** Agriculture Ditch and Reservoir Company.
**Comments:** USGS Empire quad; Elevation 11,200 feet. Non-motorized boats only.

## 39 Loch Lomond Lake

**Location:** Clear Creek County. Arapaho/Roosevelt National Forest. West on I-70 about 2 miles past Idaho Springs take exit 238, Fall River Road. Drive north on Fall River Road for 9 miles to the town of Alice. Turn left on Silver Creek and then right on Texas Drive past the "Glory Hole Mine". Take first dirt road right after the mine (rough road). Loch Lomond Lake is about 3.3 miles from Alice.
Note: Roads leading to this lake are rough unimproved dirt and/or gravel. Depending upon road conditions, a 4 wheel drive vehicle may be needed to reach the lake. Persons utilizing 2-wheel drive vehicles may have to park off road and hike to lake.
**Size:** 23 acres; 76 feet maximum depth.
**Fish:** Brook, brown and lake trout.
**Agency:** Agriculture Ditch and Reservoir Company.
**Comments:** USGS Empire quad; Elevation 11,180 feet. Boats allowed.
**Special Regulations:** The bag and possession limit for lake trout (Makinaw) is one fish, 20 inches or longer.

Picturesque Fall River Reservoir

## 40 Lake Caroline

**Location:** Clear Creek County. Arapaho/Roosevelt National Forest. West on I-70 about 2 miles past Idaho Springs . Take exit 238 - Fall River Road. Drive north on Fall River Road to the town of Alice. Turn left on Silver Creek then right on Texas Drive past the "Glory Hole Mine". Take the first dirt road right after the Glory Hole Mine (rough road) and drive to Loch Lomond. Hike west cross county for one-half mile to Lake Caroline.
**Note:** Roads leading to this lake are rough unimproved dirt and/or gravel. Depending upon road conditions , a 4-wheel drive vehicle may be needed to reach the lake. Persons utilizing 2-wheel drive vehicles may have to park off road and hike to lake.
**Size:** 8.6 acres; 58 feet maximum depth.
**Fish:** Cutthroat trout.
**Agency:** USFS-Clear Creek Ranger District.
**Comments:** USGS Empire quad; Elevation 11,840 feet. Non-motorized boats only.

## 41 Saint Mary's Lake

**Location:** Clear Creek County. Arapaho/Roosevelt National Forest. West on I-70 about 2 miles past Idaho Springs take exit 238 - Fall River Road. Drive 10 miles on Fall River Road (past the town of Alice) to St. Mary's Glacier Lodge. Park and hike northwest about one-quarter mile up an old road to Saint Mary's Lake.
**Size:** 7.2 acres; 21 feet maximum depth.
**Fish:** Brook trout.
**Agency:** USFS-Clear Creek Ranger District.
**Comments:** USGS Empire quad; Elevation 10, 710 feet. Non-motorized boats only.

## 42 Fall River Reservoir

**Location:** Clear Creek County. Arapaho/Roosevelt National Forest. West on I-70 about 2 miles past Idaho Springs take exit 238 - Fall River Road. Drive north on Fall River Road for 7.3 miles, where the main road turns uphill, take the narrow dirt road which follows the Fall River. Follow this road for 2.3 miles to the "Y" in the road. Take right fork for 2 miles to reservoir.
Note: Roads leading to this lake are rough unimproved dirt and/or gravel. Depending upon road conditions, a 4-wheel drive vehicle may be needed to reach the lake. Persons utilizing 2-wheel drive vehicles may have to park and walk to the lake.
**Size:** 17 acres; 80 feet maximum depth.
**Fish:** Rainbow and cutthroat trout.
**Agency:** Agriculture Ditch and Reservoir Company.
**Comments:** USGS Empire quad; Elevation 10,880 feet. Non-motorized boats only.

## 43 Slater Lake

**Location:** Clear Creek County. Arapaho/Roosevelt National Forest. West on I-70 about 2 miles past Idaho Springs take exit 238 - Fall River Road. Drive north on Fall River Road for 7.3 miles, where the main road turns uphill, take the narrow dirt road which follows the Fall River. Follow this road for 2.3 miles to "Y" in the road. Take left fork (rough road) 1.2 miles to Chinn's Lake. Stay on left side of dam and go .1 mile to Sherwin Lake. Then from the northwest side of Sherwin Lake follow the stream and hike one-quarter mile to the lake.

**Note:** Roads leading to this lake are rough unimproved dirt and/or gravel. Depending upon road conditions, a 4-wheel drive vehicle may be needed to reach the lake. Persons utilizing 2-wheel drive vehicles may have to park and walk to the lake.
**Size:** 7.2 acres; 4.5 feet maximum depth.
**Fish:** Cutthroat trout.
**Agency:** USFS - Clear Creek Ranger District.
**Comments:** USGS Empire quad; Elevation 11,440 feet. Non-motorized boats only.

## 44 Sherwin Lake

**Location:** Clear Creek County. Arapaho/Roosevelt National Forest. West on I-70 about 2 miles past Idaho Springs take exit 238 - Fall River Road. Drive north on Fall River Road for 7.3 miles, where the main road turns uphill, take the narrow dirt road which follows the Fall River. Follow this road for 2.3 miles to "Y" in the road. Take left fork (rough road) 1.2 miles to Chinn's Lake. Stay on left side of dam and go .1 mile to Lake.
Note: Roads leading to this lake are rough unimproved dirt and/or gravel. Depending upon road conditions, a 4-wheel drive vehicle may be needed to reach the lake. Persons utilizing 2-wheel drive vehicles may have to park and walk to the lake.
**Size:** 8.6 acres; 21 feet maximum depth.
**Fish:** Brook, rainbow, cutthroat trout and splake.
**Agency:** USFS - Clear Creek Ranger District.
**Comments:** USGS Empire quad; Elevation 11,090 feet. Non-motorized boats only.
**Special Regulations:** Bag and possession limit for splake is 2 fish, 16 inches or longer. Artificial flies and lures only.

## 45 Chinn's Lake

**Location:** Clear Creek County. Arapaho/Roosevelt National Forest. West on I-70 about 2 miles past Idaho Springs take exit 238 - Fall River Road. Drive north on Fall River Road for 7.3 miles, where the main road turns uphill, take the narrow dirt road which follows the Fall River. Follow this road for 2.3 miles to "Y" in the road. Take left fork (rough road) 1.2 miles to Chinn's Lake.
Note: Roads leading to this lake are rough unimproved dirt and/or gravel. Depending upon road conditions, a 4-wheel drive vehicle may be needed to reach the lake. Persons utilizing 2-wheel drive vehicles may have to park and walk to the lake.
**Size:** 10 acres; 30 feet maximum depth.
**Fish:** Rainbow trout and splake.
**Agency:** USFS - Clear Creek Ranger District.
**Comments:** USGS Empire quad; Elevation 11,000 feet. Non-motorized boats only.

**Old cabin on Chinn's Lake**

## 46 Bill Moore Lake

**Location:** Clear Creek County. Arapaho/Roosevelt National Forest. From Empire, drive north on Empire Creek Road to the abandoned Conqueror Mine. Hike north and northwest on the winding 4WD road. Total distance is about 6 miles to Bill Moore Lake from Empire.
**Size:** 7 acres; 3 feet maximum depth.
**Fish:** Cutthroat trout.
**Agency:** USFS - Clear Creek Ranger District.
**Comments:** USGS Empire quad; Elevation 11,280 feet. Non-motorized boats only.

## 47 Byron Lake

**Location:** Clear Creek County. Arapaho/Roosevelt National Forest. From Empire, drive north on Empire Creek Road to the abandoned Conqueror Mine. Hike north and northwest on the winding 4WD road. Total distance is about 6 miles to Bill Moore Lake from Empire. From the northwest side of Bill Moore Lake, follow the inlet stream and take the north fork and hike 1 mile (no trail) following the stream to Byron Lake. No trail, use topo map advised.
**Size:** 2.8 acres; 9 feet maximum depth.
**Fish:** Cutthroat trout.
**Agency:** USFS - Clear Creek Ranger District.
**Comments:** USGS Empire quad; Elevation 12,100 feet. Non-motorized boats only.

## 50 Urad Reservoir - Upper

**Location:** Clear Creek County. Arapaho/Roosevelt National Forest. From Empire go about 7 miles west on US 40 to Big Ben Picnic Ground. Go a short distance and turn south, drive 2 miles on dirt road to Urad Reservoir.
**Size:** 31 acres; 48 feet maximum depth.
**Fish:** Brook, rainbow (catchable size stocked) and brown trout.
**Agency:** Amax, Inc.

Dam between Chinn's and Sherwin Lakes

## 48 Ethel Lake

**Location:** Clear Creek County. Arapaho/Roosevelt National Forest. From Empire, drive north on Empire Creek Road to the abandoned Conqueror Mine. Hike north and northwest on the winding 4WD road. Total distance is about 6 miles to Bill Moore Lake from Empire. From the northwest side of Bill Moore Lake, follow the inlet stream and take the south fork and hike west 1.2 miles following the stream to Ethel Lake. No trail, use of topo map advised.
**Size:** 5 acres; 65 feet maximum depth.
**Fish:** Cutthroat trout.
**Agency:** USFS - Clear Creek Ranger District.
**Comments:** USGS Empire quad; Elevation 12,560 feet. Non-motorized boats only.

## 49 Cone Lake

**Location:** Clear Creek County. Arapaho/Roosevelt National Forest. From Empire, drive west on US40. Follow the highway to the summit of Berthoud Pass. Hike 2 miles east on trail to Cone Lake.
**Size:** 3 acres; 8 feet maximum depth.
**Fish:** Cutthroat trout.
**Agency:** USFS - Clear Creek Ranger District.
**Comments:** USGS Berthoud Pass quad; Elevation 11,600 feet. Steep hiking. Non-motorized boats only.

**Comments:** USGS Gray's Peak quad; Elevation 10,720 feet. Mizpaw Campground is 1.5 miles up US 40 from Big Ben. No boats allowed.

## 51 Hassell Lake

**Location:** Clear Creek County. Arapaho/Roosevelt National Forest. From Empire go about 7 miles west on US 40 to Big Ben Picnic Ground. Go west from hairpin turn onto Henderson Mine road. Go a short distance and turn south, drive 2 miles on dirt road to Urad Reservoir. Hike one-half mile northwest from the reservoir along tributary stream to Hassell Lake.
**Size:** 8.6 acres; 7 feet maximum depth.
**Fish:** Brook trout.
**Agency:** USFS - Clear Creek Ranger District.
**Comments:** USGS Gray's Peak quad; Elevation 11,360 feet. Mizpaw Campground is 1.5 miles up US 40 from Big Ben. Non-motorized boats only.

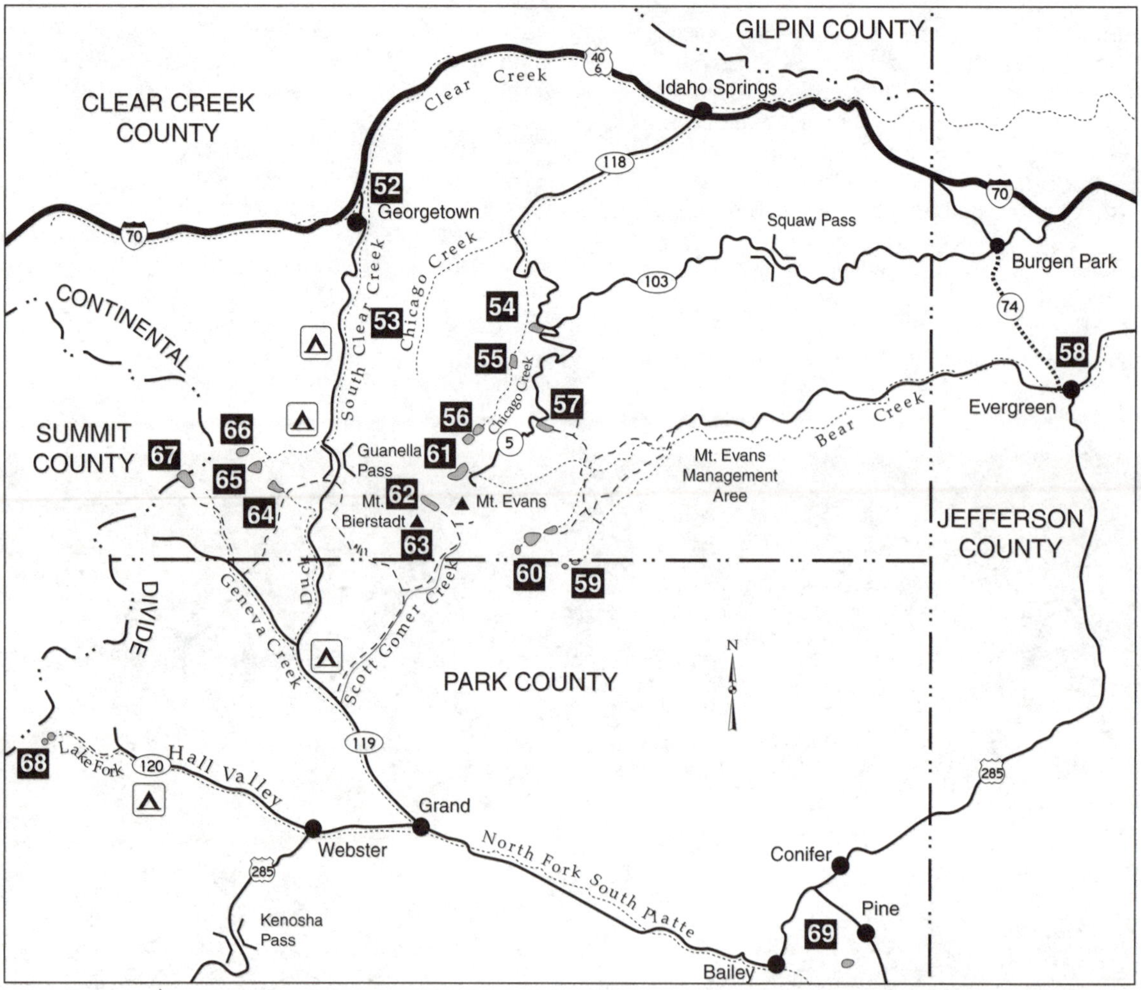
GILPIN COUNTY
CLEAR CREEK COUNTY
Clear Creek
Idaho Springs
Georgetown
Squaw Pass
Burgen Park
CONTINENTAL
DIVIDE
South Clear Creek
Chicago Creek
SUMMIT COUNTY
Guanella Pass
Mt. Bierstadt
Mt. Evans
Evergreen
Bear Creek
Mt. Evans Management Aree
JEFFERSON COUNTY
Geneva Creek
Duck
Scott Gomer Creek
PARK COUNTY
Lake Fork
Hall Valley
Grand
Webster
North Fork South Platte
Conifer
Pine
Kenosha Pass
Bailey
52
53
54
55
56
57
58
59
60
61
62
63
64
65
66
67
68
69

SECTION 3 - MAP 5

## 52 Georgetown Lake

**Location:** Clear Creek County. Arapaho/Roosevelt National Forest. From Idaho Springs, continue west on I-70 to Georgetown exit. Go south to first stop sign, turn east and drive to the lake.
**Size:** 54.3 acres; 11 feet maximum depth.
**Fish:** Rainbow trout (catchable sized stocked), brown, cutthroat and brook trout.
**Agency:** City of Georgetown.
**Comments:** USGS Georgetown quad; Elevation 8,460 feet. Clear Lake Campground is 4 miles south on Guanella Pass Road. Non-motorized boats only. Handicapped accessible fishing pier. Bighorn sheep viewing. Ice fishing.

## 53 Clear Lake

**Location:** Clear Creek County. Arapaho/Roosevelt National Forest. From Georgetown, drive south on Guanella Pass Road about 4 miles. Clear Lake is just east of the road.
**Size:** 24 acres; 98 feet maximum depth.
**Fish:** Rainbow (catchable size stocked), brook trout and sucker.

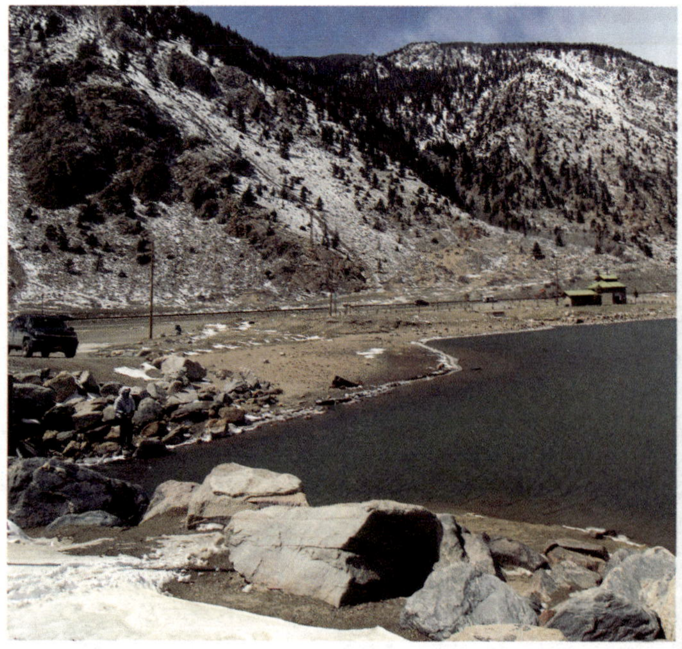

Georgetown Lake

Evergreen Lake

**Agency:** Public Service Company.
**Comments:** USGS Idaho Springs quad; Elevation 9,873 feet. Clear Lake campground is about 1 mile south of the lake. No boats.

## 54 Echo Lake

**Location:** Clear Creek County. Arapaho/Roosevelt National Forest. From Idaho Springs drive south 12 miles on Hwy 103. Lake is south of the highway just west of Mt. Evans Road.
**Size:** 18.2 acres; 7 feet maximum depth.
**Fish:** Rainbow trout (catchable size stocked).
**Agency:** Denver Parks & Recreation.
**Comments:** USGS Idaho Springs quad; Elevation 10,720 feet. West Chicago Creek Campground is 8 miles west (Reservations suggested). No boats.

## 55 Idaho Springs Reservoir

**Location:** Clear Creek County. Arapaho/Roosevelt National Forest. From Idaho Springs, drive south on Hwy 103 about 8 miles (past the Chicago Forks Picnic Grounds) to Chicago Creek Road drive south 1.5 miles and then hike 1.5 miles south on road to reservoir.
**Size:** 20 acres; 30 feet maximum depth.
**Fish:** Brook, rainbow, cutthroat trout and sucker.
**Agency:** City of Idaho Springs.
**Comments:** USGS Idaho Springs quad; Elevation 10,600 feet. West Chicago Creek Campground is 8 miles west (Reservations suggested). No boats.

## 56 Chicago Lakes

**Location:** Clear Creek County. Arapaho/Roosevelt National Forest. From Idaho Springs, drive south on Hwy 103 about 8 miles (past the Chicago Forks Picnic Grounds) to Chicago Creek Road drive south 1.5 miles and then hike 1.5 miles south on road to Idaho Springs Reservoir. Hike around the west side of the reservoir and follow the creek upstream. Go 2 miles south to Chicago Lakes. Alternate route from Idaho Springs, drive 12 miles south on Hwy 103 to Echo Lake. Hike west on Chicago Reservoir trail to Chicago Creek road, then continue as above.
**Size:** Upper Lake - 10 acres; 41 feet maximum depth. Lower Lake - 26 acres; 74 feet maximum depth.
**Fish:** Cutthroat and rainbow trout.
**Agency:** USFS - Clear Creek Ranger District.
**Comments:** USGS Idaho Springs and Mt. Evans quads; Elevation 11,620 feet. Camping at West Chicago Creek Campground (Reservations suggested). Non-motorized boats only. Located in Mount Evans Wilderness.

## 57 Lincoln Lake

**Location:** Clear Creek County. Arapaho/Roosevelt National Forest. From Idaho Springs, drive 12 miles south on Hwy 103 to Echo Lake. Hike 1 mile east on Beaverdam Trail #46. Turn south and hike over 3 miles to next fork. Turn west and hike over one-half mile on Trail #45 to Lincoln Lake.
**Size:** 12.8 acres; 61 feet maximum depth.
**Fish:** Brook, Lake trout and sucker.
**Agency:** USFS - Clear Creek Ranger District.
**Comments:** USGS Harris Park quad; Elevation 11,620 feet. Very difficult hike. Lies some 900 vertical feet directly below Mt. Evans road, 3.5 miles south of Echo Lake junction. Non-motorized boats only.

## 58 Evergreen Lake

**Location:** Jefferson County. From Denver, go west on I-70 to Evergreen Parkway exit. Go south on Hwy 74 to Evergreen. The lake is south on Hwy 74 and upper Bear Creek Road.
**Size:** 42 acres; 22 feet maximum depth.
**Fish:** Brown and rainbow trout (catchable size stocked), sucker, tiger muskie and splake.
**Agency:** City of Evergreen Park & Recreation District.
**Comments:** USGS Evergreen quad; Elevation 7,072 feet. Boating by evergreen permit only - No power boats. Open late may. Hours 5 a.m. to 10 p.m. for fishing only. Handicapped accessible fishing pier and marsh viewing boardwalk. Parking available above and below dam.

Summit Lake at 12,900 feet

## 59 Roosevelt Lakes

**Location:** Park County. Arapaho/Roosevelt National Forest. From Denver, drive south on US 285. Near the top of Crow Hill, 3 miles north of Bailey, turn northwest on Forest Route 100. Drive about 9 miles to Deer Creek Campground, the end of the road. Hike north 4 miles on Tanglewood Creek Trail #636 to Roosevelt Lakes. From Evergreen, drive about 6 miles west on upper Bear Creek Road. Take the west fork after Brookvale, and continue west for 2 miles. Take the south fork, go 2 miles and take the north fork. Continue west for 4 miles to Camp Rock Trailhead. Hike about 4.5 miles southwest on Beartrack Lakes Trail #43, to Beartrack Lakes. From here hike one mile southeast on trail #78 to Roosevelt Lakes.
**Size:** 2 lakes; 6 acres total; 22 feet maximum depth.
**Fish:** Cutthroat, rainbow and brook trout.
**Agency:** USFS - Clear Creek Ranger District.
**Comments:** USGS Harris Park quad; Elevation 10,400 feet. Located in Mount Evans Wilderness. Non-motorized boats only.

## 60 Beartrack Lakes

**Location:** Clear Creek County. Arapaho/Roosevelt National Forest. From Denver, go west on I-70 to Evergreen Parkway exit. Go south on Hwy 74 to Evergreen. From Evergreen drive about 6 miles west on Upper Bear Creek Road. Take the west fork after Brookvale, and continue west for 2 miles. Take the south fork, go 2 miles then take the north fork. Continue west for 4 miles to Camp Rock Trailhead. Hike about 4.5 miles southwest on Beartrack Lakes Trail #43, to the lakes.
**Size:** Upper Lake - 5 acres; 25 feet maximum depth.
Lower Lake - 11 acres; 28 feet maximum depth.
**Fish:** Brook and cutthroat trout.
**Agency:** USFS - Clear Creek Ranger District.
**Comments:** USGS Harris Park quad; Elevation 10,500 feet. Camping at Beartrack Lakes and Echo Lake Campground. Follow trail signs. Dogs must be on 6 foot leash in elk management area. Located in Mount Evans Wilderness. Non-motorized boats only.

## 61 Summit Lake

**Location:** Clear Creek County. Arapaho/Roosevelt National Forest. From Idaho Springs, drive 12 miles south on Hwy 103 to Echo Lake. East of the Lake turn south on Mt. Evans road, Hwy 5. Drive 9 miles, the lake is just west of the road.
**Size:** 32.8 acres; 70 feet maximum depth.
**Fish:** Rainbow and cutthroat trout.
**Agency:** Denver Parks & Recreation.
**Comments:** USGS Mt. Evans quad; Elevation 12,900 feet. Roadside fishery. Non-motorized boats only.
Open 5 a.m. to 11 p.m.

## 62 Abyss Lake

**Location:** Clear Creek County. Pike National Forest. From Grant, drive north on Guanella Pass Road (Forest Route 118) to Burning Bear Campground. Hike 3.5 miles northeast on Scott Gomer Creek Trail to Lake Fork Trail #602. (Just past Deer Creek Trail #603.) Hike northeast 3 miles on Lake Fork Trail to Abyss Lake. From Georgetown, drive south on Guanella Pass Road. Drive about 6 miles from the summit of the pass to Burning Bear Campground and continue as above. Abyss Lake is between Mt. Evans and Mt. Bierstadt.
**Size:** 18 acres; 50 feet maximum depth.
**Fish:** Rainbow and cutthroat trout.
**Agency:** USFS - South Platte Ranger District.
**Comments:** USGS Mt. Evans quad; Elevation 12,640 feet. Frozen over until mid-June or later. Harsh environment. Camping at Burning Bear and Geneva Park Campgrounds. Non-motorized boats only. Located in Mount Evans Wilderness.

## 63 Frozen Lake

**Location:** Clear Creek County. Pike National Forest. From Grant, drive north on Guanella Pass Road (Forest Route 118) to Burning Bear Campground. Hike 3.5 miles northeast on Scott Gomer Creek Trail to Lake Fork Trail, past 2 trails going east, and continue 1 mile north on Scott Gomer. Follow the creek north where the trail heads west. Hike 2 miles upstream to Frozen Lake. Rugged terrain, use of topo map advised. From Georgetown, drive south on Guanella Pass Road. Drive about 6 miles south from the summit of the pass to Burning Bear Campground. Continue as above.
**Size:** 7 acres; 33 feet maximum depth.
**Fish:** Cutthroat trout.
**Agency:** USFS - South Platte Ranger District.
**Comments:** USGS Mt. Evans quad; Elevation 12,960 feet. Harsh environment. Lake is frozen over until mid-June or later. Mt. Bierstadt, 14,060 feet, looms over the lake. Camping at Burning Bear and Geneva Park Campgrounds. No boats. Located in Mount Evans Wilderness.

## 64 Square Top Lakes

**Location:** Clear Creek County. Arapaho/Roosevelt National Forest. From Georgetown, drive south on Guanella Pass Road to the summit of the pass. Hike 2 miles west on the trail to Square Top Lakes.
**Size:** 2 lakes; 10 acres each.
**Fish:** Cutthroat trout.
**Agency:** USFS - Clear Creek Ranger District.
**Comments:** USGS Mt. Evans quad; Elevation 12,160 feet. Guanella Pass and Clear Lake Campgrounds nearby on the south fork of Clear Creek. Non-motorized boats only.

## 65 Silver Dollar Lake

**Location:** Clear Creek County. Arapaho/Roosevelt National Forest. From Georgetown, go 7 miles south on Guanella Pass Road to Guanella Pass Campground. Just pass the campground take the west fork. Drive one mile to Naylor Lake (which is private). Hike west along the south side of Taylor Lake to a trail along the creek. Hike one half mile west along the west fork of the trail to Silver Dollar Lake. From Grant, drive north on Forest Route 118, Guanella Pass Road, over the pass to Guanella Pass Campground. Continue from campground as in above directions.
**Size:** 18.6 acres; 73 feet maximum depth.
**Fish:** Cutthroat trout.
**Agency:** USFS - Clear Creek Ranger District

Pine Valley Ranch Pond

**Comments:** USGS Mt. Evans and Montezuma quads; Elevation 11,950 feet. Non-motorized boats only.

## 66 Murray Lake

**Location:** Clear Creek County. Arapaho/Roosevelt National Forest. From Georgetown, go 7 miles south on Guanella Pass Road to Guanella Pass Campground. Just pass the campground take the west fork. Drive one mile to Naylor Lake (which is private). Hike west along the south side of Naylor Lake, to a trail along the creek. Hike 1 mile northwest on the north fork of the trail to Murray Lake.
**Size:** 11.4 acres; 38 feet maximum depth.
**Fish:** Cutthroat trout.
**Agency:** USFS - Clear Creek Ranger District.
**Comments:** USGS Mt. Evans and Montezuma quads; Elevation 12,080 feet. Non-motorized boats only.

## 67 Shelf Lake

**Location:** Clear Creek County. Pike National Forest. From Grant, drive north on Guanella Pass Road, Forest Route 118, to Duck Creek Picnic Ground. Take the west fork of the road. Drive 3 miles northwest up Geneva Creek Road, Forest Route 119, to Smelter Gulch. Hike 3 miles up the trail to Shelf Lake.
**Size:** 9.5 acres; 40 feet maximum depth.
**Fish:** Cutthroat trout.
**Agency:** USFS - South Platte Ranger District.
**Comments:** USGS Montezuma quad; Elevation 12,000 feet. Harsh environment. Lake is frozen over until mid-June or later. Mt. Bierstadt, 14,060 feet, looms over the lake. Camping at Burning Bear and Geneva Creek Campgrounds. Non-motorized boats only.

## 68 Gibson Lake

**Location:** Park County. Pike National Forest. From Denver, drive south on US 285 and turn north on Webster. Drive 7 miles northwest on Hall Valley Road, Forest Route 120, to trailhead at Gibson Lake Trail Picnic Ground. Hike 2.5 miles south and then west on Gibson Lake Trail #633.
**Size:** 3 acres; 23 feet maximum depth.
**Fish:** Brook trout.
**Agency:** USFS - South Platte Ranger District.
**Comments:** USGS Jefferson quad; 11,500 feet. Hall Valley Campground near trailhead. Non-motorized boats only.

## 69 Pine Valley Ranch Pond

**Location:** Access via U. S. Highway 285 south to Pine Junction, turn south (left) at Pine Junction onto Colo. 126 and follow southeast 5.6 miles to the turn-off for Pine Valley Ranch Park (Jefferson County Open Space) - before the town of Pine. Follow this road west approximately 1 miles to the Visitors Center parking lot. Cross the North Fork of the South Platte River via the foot bridge and follow the trail to the pond. Access to the North Fork of the South Platte River and many hiking trails.
**Size:** 8 acres; 10 feet maximum depth.
**Fish:** Rainbow (catchable-size stocked), brown trout and sucker.
**Agency:** Jefferson County Open Space.
**Comments:** Excellent access to many hiking trails and picnic area. Visitors center and restrooms located near parking lot. Handicapped-accessible stream and pond piers.
**Special Regulations:** Four trout bag and possession limit in the park (stream and pond combined); children under 16 without a license - 2 trout bag and possession limit in the park (stream and pond combined).

## Section 4

# Six Streams Near the Metro Area

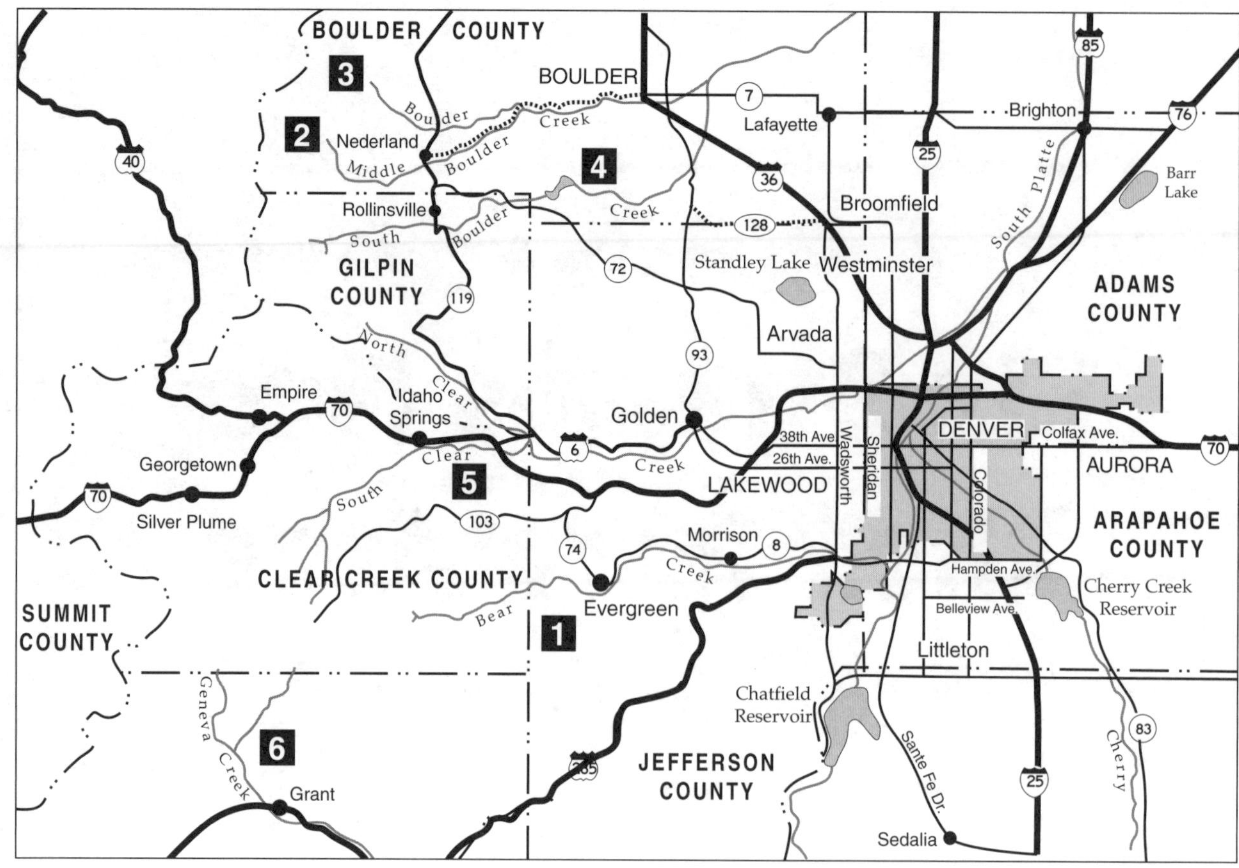


SECTION 4 - MAP 1

## 1 Bear Creek

**Location:** Clear Creek and Jefferson counties. Headwaters on Mt. Evans, flows easterly through the Denver Metro area to the South Platte River.
**Fish:** Rainbow, brown, cutthroat and brook trout.
Nearby Lakes: Lincoln Lakes, Beartrack Lakes, Evergreen Lake and Bear Creek Reservoir.
**Comments:** Headwaters are in Arapaho National Forest with the upper reaches accessible only by foot or horseback from Mt. Evans Road. or along the Creek west of Evergreen. Some private property in developed areas. East of Morrison the creek often runs through public green belt areas.

## 2 Boulder Creek-Middle

**Location:** Boulder County. Flows easterly from the Continental Divide west of Nederland (Hwy 72) to Barker Reservoir into Boulder Canyon (Hwy 119) to merge with north Boulder Creek to form Boulder Creek which flows through Boulder.
**Fish:** Rainbow, brown cutthroat and brook trout.
**Nearby Lakes:** King Lake, Skyscraper Reservoir, Devil's Thumb Lake, Jasper Lake, Diamond Lake, Lake Dorothy, Banana Lake, Upper Diamond Lake, Lost Lake, Betty Lake, Bob Lake, Woodland Lake, Storm Lake, and Glacier Lake.
**Comments:** Headwaters in Roosevelt National Forest are

**Fishing access for Bear Creek in Bear Creek Lake Park**

open to the public. Major portions of stream are private and posted. Upper reaches of the south fork of Middle Boulder Creek are in the Indian Peaks Wilderness Area and are accessible by foot or horseback only. The forks join 1.5 miles west of Eldora at Hessie east of Barker Reservoir Hwy 119 is adjacent to the creek in Boulder Canyon. Fishing possible in the city of Boulder.
**Special Regulations**: From Upper end of Ebin Fine Park to 55th Street, fishing is by artificial flies or lures only. All fish caught must be returned to the water immediately (Catch and release only).

**Clear Creek in Prospect Park**

## 3 Boulder Creek-North

**Location:** Boulder County. Flows southwesterly from its headwaters in the lakes at the foot of Arapaho Glacier northwest of Nederland along the Continental Divide.
**Fish:** Rainbow, cutthroat and brook trout.
**Nearby Lakes:** Rainbow Lakes.
**Comments:** The creek and associated lakes are on a mixture of public and private property in Arapaho/Roosevelt National Forest. Best fishing in the area is at Rainbow Lakes where there is Rainbow Lakes Campground and trailhead for going to the Glacier.

## 4 Boulder Creek-South

**Location:** Gilpin and Boulder Counties. Flows easterly from the Continental Divide west of Rollinsville (Hwy 72) to Gross Reservoir, Eldorado Canyon State Park, and through Boulder.
**Fish:** Rainbow, brook, cutthroat and brown trout.
Nearby Lakes: James Peak Lake, Roger' s Pass Lake, Heart Lake, Iceberg Lakes, Clayton Lake, Crater Lake, Arapaho Lakes, Forest Lakes, Gross Reservoir, Jenny Lake, and Yankee Doodle Lake.
**Comments:** Headwaters in Roosevelt National Forest are open to the public. Sections of the stream are on posted private property, portions are channeled west of Rollinsville. Between Pine Cliffe an Eldorado Canyon State Park terrain is extremely rugged and access is difficult. Below the park, 8 miles southeast of Boulder, a mile-long stretch of the stream on the Walker Ranch is open to public fishing. Take Flagstaff Drive from Boulder parking area and hike one mile to the creek.

## 5 Clear Creek

**Location:** Clear Creek and Jefferson Counties. Flows easterly from the Continental Divide near the Eisenhower Tunnel along I-70 at the foot of Loveland Pass and into the Denver Metro area. The most fishable portions are adjacent to highways and frontage roads. There is some private property.
**Fish:** Rainbow, brook, cutthroat and brown trout.
Nearby Lakes: Silver Dollar Lake, Murray Lake, Georgetown Lake, Hassel Lake, Ethel Lake, Bill Moore Lake, Chinn's Lake, Sherwin Lake, Slater Lake, Fall River Reservoir, Reynolds Lake, Steuart Lake, Loch Lomond Lake, Lake Caroline, Ice Lake, St. Mary's Lake, Prospect Park Lakes, Summit Lake, Idaho Springs Reservoir, Echo Lake.
**Comments:** Headwaters are in Arapaho/Roosevelt National Forest. Streams tributary to Clear Creek (including Chicago Creek, the South Fork of Clear Creek, and the headwaters reaches of the North and West Forks of Clear Creek) support populations of rainbow, brook and cutthroat trout.

## 6 Geneva Creek

**Location:** Park and Clear Creek counties. Flows southerly into the north fork of the South Platte River at Grant on US 285.
**Fish:** Rainbow, brown, cutthroat and brook trout.
Nearby Lakes: Shelf Lake, Square Top Lakes, Abyss Lakes, and Frozen Lake.
**Comments:** Headwaters to Scott Gomer Creek in Pike National Forest have insignificant fish populations. Below the falls at Burning Bear Campground is intermittent public and private land. Tributary streams have small brook trout. Camping is at Burning Bear and Geneva Park Campgrounds and underdeveloped sites upstream from Guanella Pass junction. Good road parallels most of the stream.

## Section 5

# The South Platte River

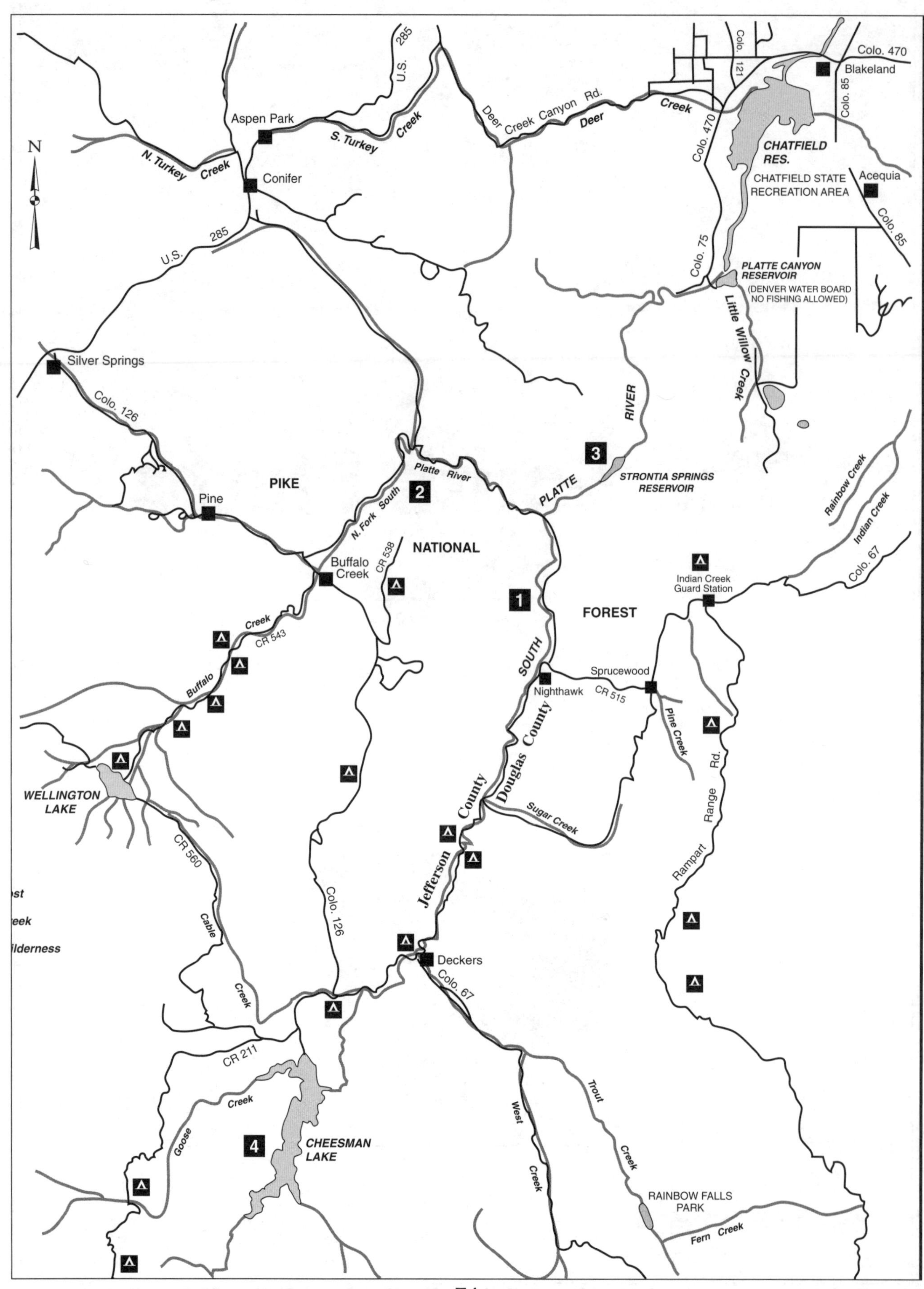
N
N. Turkey Creek
Aspen Park
S. Turkey Creek
U.S. 285
Conifer
Deer Creek Canyon Rd.
Deer Creek
Colo. 121
Colo. 470
Blakeland
Colo. 85
CHATFIELD RES.
CHATFIELD STATE RECREATION AREA
Acequia
Colo. 75
PLATTE CANYON RESERVOIR
(DENVER WATER BOARD NO FISHING ALLOWED)
Little Willow Creek
Silver Springs
Colo. 126
PIKE
Pine
Platte River
N. Fork South
NATIONAL
Buffalo Creek
CR 538
RIVER
PLATTE
STRONTIA SPRINGS RESERVOIR
Rainbow Creek
Indian Creek
Colo. 67
Indian Creek Guard Station
FOREST
SOUTH
Sprucewood
Nighthawk
CR 515
Pine Creek
Rampart Range Rd.
Buffalo Creek
CR 543
WELLINGTON LAKE
Douglas County
Jefferson County
Sugar Creek
CR 560
Cable Creek
Colo. 126
Deckers
Colo. 67
CR 211
Goose Creek
CHEESMAN LAKE
West Creek
Trout Creek
RAINBOW FALLS PARK
Fern Creek
1
2
3
4

## 1 South Platte River

**Location:** Park, Jefferson, Douglas, and Denver counties. The river enters the area discussed in this guide at Chessman Reservoir - at the juncture of Teller, Douglas, Jefferson, and Park counties about 45 miles Southwest of Denver. Flows northeasterly through Denver.
**Fish:** Brown, rainbow, and brook trout.
Comments: The South Platte flows through Pike National Forest until it reaches the outskirts of the Denver metro area. In some mountain stretches it is a premier year-round trout stream. Upper portion of the river is accessible via Hwy 67 west from Sedalia, north from Woodland Park, or south from US 285 on Jefferson County roads at Kennedy Gulch, Shaffers Crossing, and Pine Junction. Below Cheesman Lake the river is dammed at Strontia Springs in South Platte River Canyon. The stretch of river through Waterton Canyon (between Strontia Springs and Chatfield) is reached via walk-in access from Kassler Treatment Plant. Below Chatfield, fishing for stocked trout or warm water fish is available on the river through much of the Denver area.
**Special Regulations:** From Cheesman Dam downstream to the Upper Wigwam property line: 1. Fishing by artificial flies or artificial lures only; 2. All fish caught must be returned to the water immediately (catch & release only). From the lower boundary of the Wigwam Club to Scraggy View Campground: 1. Fishing by artificial flies or artificial lures only; 2. Bag, possession, and size limit four trout is 2 fish, 15 inches or longer. From Scraggy View Picnic Ground downstream to and including Strontia Springs Reservoir; The Bag and possession limit for trout is 2 fish. From Strontia Springs Dam downstream to 300 yards upstream from the Denver Water Board's diversion structure. l. Fishing by artificial flies or artificial lures (except that only naturally including aquatic nymphs and/or larvae in the South Platte River are permitted as bait); 2. Bag, possession, and size limit for trout is 2 fish, 16 inches or longer.

South Platte River

## 2 South Platte River - North Fork

**Location:** Park and Jefferson counties. Flows southeasterly from near Webster and Kenosha passes, along US 285. Most of the river course has been modified by construction and additional water surging in from the Harold G. Roberts Tunnel at Grant. At Bailey, the highway curves north, leaving the river, most of which is on private property until it reaches the South Platte River.
**Fish:** Rainbow, cutthroat, and brown trout.
Nearby Lakes: Gibson Lake, Abyss Lake, Frozen Lake, Square Top Lakes, Shelf Lake, Beartrack Lake, and Roosevelt Lake.
**Comments:** Most of the North Fork of the South Platte River is on private land with only limited public fishing opportunity. Public access is greater on segments closer to the North Fork confluence with the South Platte River. Headwaters in Pike National Forest are small, often brushy mountain streams.
**Special Regulations:** All wipers possessed must be 15 inches or longer.

## 3 Strontia Springs Reservoir

**Location:** Jefferson and Douglas counties. From Denver, go south on Hwy 75 (west of Chatfield Recreation Area) to Kassler. Hike 6.2 miles southwest on the road

going up along the South Platte River. Rough terrain. From Deckers, go north on Hwy 67 about 12 miles, alongside the South Platte River, where the North Fork meets the South Platte. Park and hike in to the south end of the reservoir.
**Size:** 118 acres; 212 feet maximum depth.
**Fish:** Rainbow trout, (catchable size stocked), sucker, tiger muskie, northern pike and kokanee salmon.
**Agency:** Denver Water Department.

Vegetation around Cheesman Lake still shows effects of the June 2002 Hayman fire

**Comments:** USGS Platte Canyon quad; Elevation 5,900 feet. No ice fishing. Fluctuating reservoir. No boats or floating devices.
**Special Regulations:** The bag and possession limit for trout is 2 fish.

## 4 Cheesman Lake

**Location:** Douglas and Jefferson counties. Pike National Forest. From Denver, drive west on US 285 to Pine Junction. Turn south (to Pine) on County Road 126, drive about 20 miles south to Forest Route 211, and turn west. Go west 1 mile, the road turns south. Go 1.5 miles to the lake. Alternate route from Denver, drive south on US 85 to Sedalia. Turn southwest on Hwy 67, follow 67 through several intersections (4) to Deckers. Drive 3 miles west on County Road 126. Continue west on Forest Route 211 for 1 mile. Road turns south, go 1.5 miles to lake.
**Size:** 875 acres; 190 feet maximum depth.
**Fish:** Rainbow, brown and brook trout, northern pike, smallmouth bass, sucker, splake, lake trout, kokanee salmon and yellow perch.
**Agency:** Denver Water Department.
**Comments:** USGS- Cheesman Lake quad; Elevation 7,425 feet. Shore fishing only. Walk-in from parking area on north end. Restrooms.
**Special Regulations:** 1. Ice fishing prohibited; 2. Boating and floating devices prohibited; 3. Fishing is prohibited from one-half hour after sunset until one-half hour before sunrise; 4. Fishing is prohibited from the dam, and as posted; (No access on or across dam); 6. Spear fishing equipment is prohibited; 5. Fishing is prohibited January 1, through April 30; 6. Kokanee snagging permitted September 1 through December 31.
**Note:** In waters open to snagging, all snagged fish, except Kokanee salmon, must be returned to the water immediately.
**Special Note:** Scheduled to reopen summer 2007. Call ahead for access information.

# Index